# The Workbook for Healing Developmental Trauma

# THE WORKBOOK FOR

# HEALING DEVELOPMENTAL TRAUMA

## Tools and Techniques from the NeuroAffective Relational Model (NARM)

Laurence Heller, PhD, and Brad J. Kammer, LMFT, LPCC

North Atlantic Books
Huichin, unceded Ohlone land
Berkeley, California

North Atlantic Books
Huichin, unceded Ohlone land
2526 Martin Luther King Jr Way
Berkeley, CA 94704 USA
www.northatlanticbooks.com

Cover design by Howie Severson
Book design by Happenstance Type-O-Rama
Graphics design by Amanda Losch

Printed in the United States of America

The Workbook for Healing Developmental Trauma: Tools and Techniques from the NeuroAffective Relational Model (NARM) is sponsored and published by North Atlantic Books, an educational nonprofit based in the unceded Ohlone land Huichin (Berkeley, CA) that collaborates with partners to develop cross-cultural perspectives; nurture holistic views of art, science, the humanities, and healing; and seed personal and global transformation by publishing work on the relationship of body, spirit, and nature.

MEDICAL DISCLAIMER: The following information is intended for general information purposes only. Individuals should always see their health care provider before administering any suggestions made in this book. Any application of the material set forth in the following pages is at the reader's discretion and is their sole responsibility.

North Atlantic Books's publications are distributed to the US trade and internationally by Penguin Random House Publisher Services. For further information, visit our website at www.northatlanticbooks.com.

ISBN: 979-8-88984-287-3 (paperback) ISBN: 979-8-88984-288-0 (epub)

The authorized representative in the EU for product safety and compliance is Eucomply OÜ, Pärnu mnt 139b-14, 11317 Tallinn, Estonia, hello@eucompliancepartner.com, +33757690241.

1 2 3 4 5 6 7 8 9 KPC 30 29 28 27 26 25

# Contents

# Acknowledgments

Thank you to both of our families and those who have continued to support us.

Thank you to Amanda Losch for the creative guidance and engaging artwork.

Thank you to the team at North Atlantic Books for encouraging us to share more resources on the NeuroAffective Relational Model.

Thank you to the teams at the NARM Training Institute and the Complex Trauma Training Center for all the ways you are supporting us in bringing NARM into the world.

We are deeply grateful to our international NARM Community—the many skillful and heartful therapists we have had the pleasure to train, mentor, and collaborate with—who are committed to bringing NARM into a world that desperately needs healing.

And to everyone out there who is working to make a difference in the lives of others, we hope this workbook can lead to greater healing, health, and well-being.

# Introduction

Since publishing *The Practical Guide for Healing Developmental Trauma* in 2022, we have received numerous requests for a simple "desktop guide" to the NeuroAffective Relational Model (NARM). So we are excited to share this follow-up workbook, which is an easy-to-use manual for applying NARM skills.

This workbook presents skills that were introduced in our previous book, as well as some theoretical framework underlying the therapeutic skills. Additionally, we provide both professional and personal exercises intended to support your learning and integration of NARM.

Although this book is designed for therapists looking to expand their skills for working with complex trauma, we have also written it with a larger audience in mind, as a resource for anyone interested in healing complex trauma—professionally or personally. Readers do not need to be previously familiar with NARM. Although it is a psychologically nuanced model, we have as concisely as possible illustrated the core NARM skills.

The NeuroAffective Relational Model was introduced in the 2012 book *Healing Developmental Trauma: How Early Trauma Affects Self-Regulation, Self-Image, and the Capacity for Relationship*. Developed by Dr. Laurence Heller, NARM is one of the first clinical models specifically designed to address the impact of adverse childhood experiences (ACEs) and complex post-traumatic stress disorder (C-PTSD).

NARM draws on different models within Western psychology, as well as non-Western approaches to health and healing. NARM follows the lineage of relationally focused, depth-oriented, and neurobiologically informed psychotherapeutic models, namely psychodynamic and somatic psychotherapy. Additionally, NARM has been inspired and shaped by various cultural, religious, and spiritual traditions. As an integrative modality, NARM works both "top-down" and "bottom-up," meaning it addresses the complex interplay of neurobiological systems that lead to a distorted sense of Self, along with dysregulated patterns of physiology, emotions, cognitions, behaviors, and interpersonal relations.

Terminology is still being debated and defined as the trauma field evolves, but we differentiate between two main categories of trauma: *shock trauma*, as articulated by PTSD (post-traumatic stress disorder), and *complex trauma*, as articulated by C-PTSD (complex post-traumatic stress disorder). The term *developmental trauma* is often used as a subset of *complex trauma* to highlight the impact of adverse childhood experiences in early life. In this workbook, we will simplify by using these two terms interchangeably.

This workbook, and NARM as a model, provides skills for specifically addressing prolonged, interpersonal forms of trauma (complex trauma), which include attachment, developmental, relational, cultural, and intergenerational trauma. The clinical approach is based on a theoretical framework that highlights the psychobiological adaptations humans must make in order to survive the impact of ACEs and other forms of relational trauma. Being relationally focused, depth-oriented, and somatic-based, NARM provides not just a clinical approach for resolving complex trauma, but a blueprint for supporting relational health.

In this workbook, we'll first review key concepts related to developmental trauma, including ACEs, C-PTSD, and post-traumatic growth. We'll give an overview of the NARM theoretical framework and, specifically, the five adaptive survival styles. We will then provide clinical guidance via the Four Pillars, the NARM Relational Model, the NARM Emotional Completion Model, and the NARM Personality Spectrum.

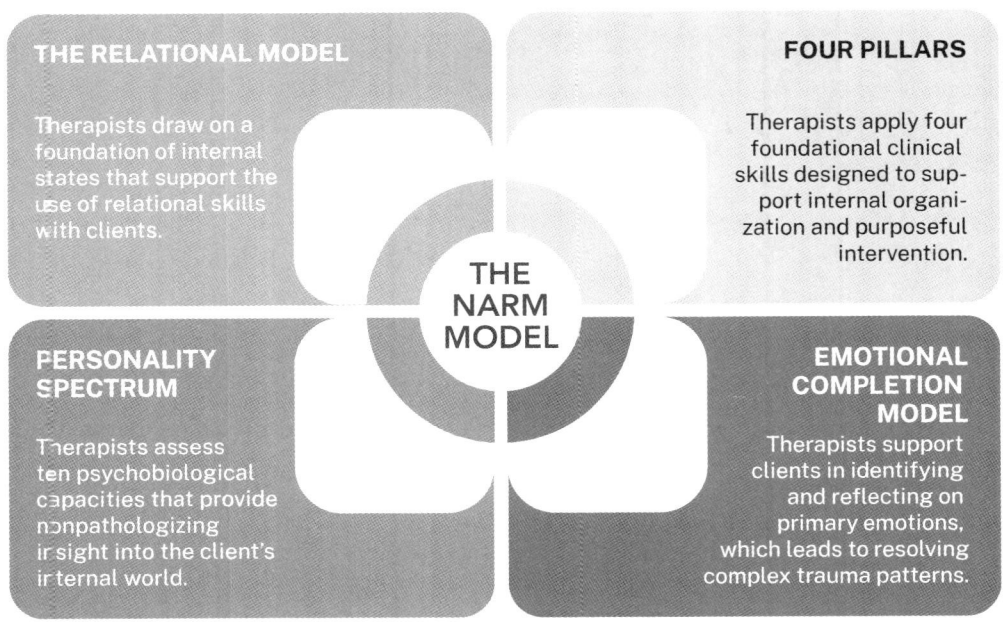

**THE RELATIONAL MODEL**

Therapists draw on a foundation of internal states that support the use of relational skills with clients.

**FOUR PILLARS**

Therapists apply four foundational clinical skills designed to support internal organization and purposeful intervention.

**THE NARM MODEL**

**PERSONALITY SPECTRUM**

Therapists assess ten psychobiological capacities that provide nonpathologizing insight into the client's internal world.

**EMOTIONAL COMPLETION MODEL**

Therapists support clients in identifying and reflecting on primary emotions, which leads to resolving complex trauma patterns.

Overview of the NARM® Model

Two sets of reflection exercises appear at the end of each section in this book, intended to provide opportunities for direct experience of NARM beyond just theoretical learning. *Personal* exercises invite reflection into your own personal relationship to the material. *Therapist-oriented* prompts invite reflection into how you might bring this material to your clients. If you are not a clinician, you are welcome to use the therapist-oriented exercises to reflect on personal relationships in your life. We invite you to take time with these reflections to digest and support integration of this complex material.

Although the NeuroAffective Relational Model is a comprehensive therapeutic approach that takes time to learn and integrate, the tips and exercises here can guide you along your way. We encourage you to keep this clinical resource handy as you bring NARM into your professional and personal life.

If this workbook inspires you to further your clinical development or personal growth, there are ways to deepen your direct, embodied experience of NARM beyond theoretical learning. Professionally, we invite eligible helping professionals to look into getting trained in NARM. Personally, we encourage anyone interested in their own healing to work with a trained NARM therapist. For information on how to locate NARM trainings and NARM therapists, see the links in the "Additional Resources" section at the end of the workbook.

The clinical guidance in this book is designed to help you deepen your effectiveness in your work, strengthening therapeutic presence and relationship. The personal reflections are intended to help you continually grow in yourself, building greater capacity for connection, health, and aliveness. It is our hope that this workbook may support you in all areas of your life.

**PERSONAL**

# Reflecting on your own personal experience

**1.**   What is it that you want for yourself in your personal growth?

**2.**   Can you identify a theme in your personal life that is unresolved and that is impacting you and your relationships?

**3.**   Can you identify some area in your life where you feel like you self-sabotage?

**THERAPIST-ORIENTED**

# Reflecting on your professional experience

1.  What is it that you want for yourself in your professional development?

2.  Can you identify a theme in your work with clients that you have difficulty with?

3.  Do you find yourself taking too much responsibility and pressuring yourself around the therapeutic process?

As you go through the different sections in this workbook, remind yourself of what you're hoping for both professionally and personally, and see how the NARM skills may support you in both areas of your life.

# ADVERSE CHILDHOOD EXPERIENCES (ACEs)

## Recognizing the impact of environmental failure and developmental trauma

**The research on adverse childhood experiences (ACEs)** has helped us conceptualize the various influences that lead to developmental trauma. Although the field of developmental trauma has largely focused on attachment and attunement failures from caregiver to child, we use the broader term *environmental failure* to capture the additional layers of discrimination, community violence, war, famine, and other forms of cultural and intergenerational trauma that negatively affect healthy child development, and ultimately lead to individual and collective suffering.

What we've learned from the ACEs research is illustrated through the ACEs pyramid: Adults who experienced persistent environmental failure in their childhood, as assessed through an ACE score, have a much higher likelihood of developing various psychological disorders such as mood, anxiety, panic, dissociative, eating, sleep, behavioral, learning, and personality disorders—as well as physical diseases such as diabetes, heart disease, strokes, autoimmune disorders, and even cancer. In addition, we see higher rates of substance abuse, domestic violence, child abuse, criminal behavior, attempted suicide, and early mortality.

## ACEs Pyramid

The ACEs Pyramid

Although recognizing the impact of environmental failure is critical to effective treatment of complex trauma, having a full history of what our clients lived through as children is not our primary focus in NARM. For example, we do not invite clients to detail their developmental trauma histories to us. Sitting with our clients, however, we organically learn a lot about the developmental challenges they experienced. And it can be helpful to have a general sense of what they believe most impacted them.

Therapists who do want to get a clearer picture of a client's early experiences can inquire about the ten types of early trauma that are in an ACE score: physical abuse, sexual abuse, psychological abuse, physical neglect, psychological neglect, witnessing domestic abuse, witnessing drug and alcohol abuse, family member with mental illness, family member incarcerated, and loss of parent through divorce, incarceration, abandonment, or death. Therapists may use questions related to these ten categories to bring greater awareness to how a client's present life may have been impacted by their early life experience. For many clients, the awareness of this impact of early trauma can be helpful in normalizing their symptoms. For therapists, this information can help provide greater context for the client's present suffering.

In NARM, whether our clients can remember their early trauma is secondary to our exploring the adaptive strategies that they developed as children to survive their environment and have carried forward into their adult lives. Learning about their adaptations to early trauma illuminates patterns of present suffering and informs our clinical direction.

**EXERCISES**

**PERSONAL**

## Reflecting on your own experience

1. How many of the ten types of early traumatic experiences (see list on p. 8) did you experience?

2. How have those adverse childhood experiences impacted you?

3. How have you learned to deal with these environmental failures?

# Reflecting with a client

1. Ask your client how many of the ten types of early traumatic experiences (listed above) they experienced in their early life.

2. Inquire into how those adverse childhood experiences have impacted them.

3. Inquire into how they have learned to deal with these environmental failures.

# COMPLEX POST-TRAUMATIC STRESS DISORDER (C-PTSD)

## *Ongoing trauma to Self*

**When the World Health Organization** released its eleventh edition of the *International Classification of Diseases*, it officially introduced complex post-traumatic stress disorder (C-PTSD) as a disorder that requires clinical treatment. C-PTSD adds three categories of symptoms to the diagnostic requirements for PTSD (post-traumatic stress disorder): *affect dysregulation*, *negative self-concept*, and *interpersonal disturbances*.

Building upon research in ACEs, as well as in the rapidly evolving field of trauma, the C-PTSD diagnosis provides a framework for identifying and understanding the suffering that our clients are experiencing as a result of unresolved attachment, developmental, relational, cultural, and intergenerational trauma.

Although there is overlap between PTSD and C-PTSD—particularly noticeable in how clients present in therapy—there are also significant theoretical differences. So it is important for mental health professionals to differentiate them clinically in order to best address the full spectrum of trauma.

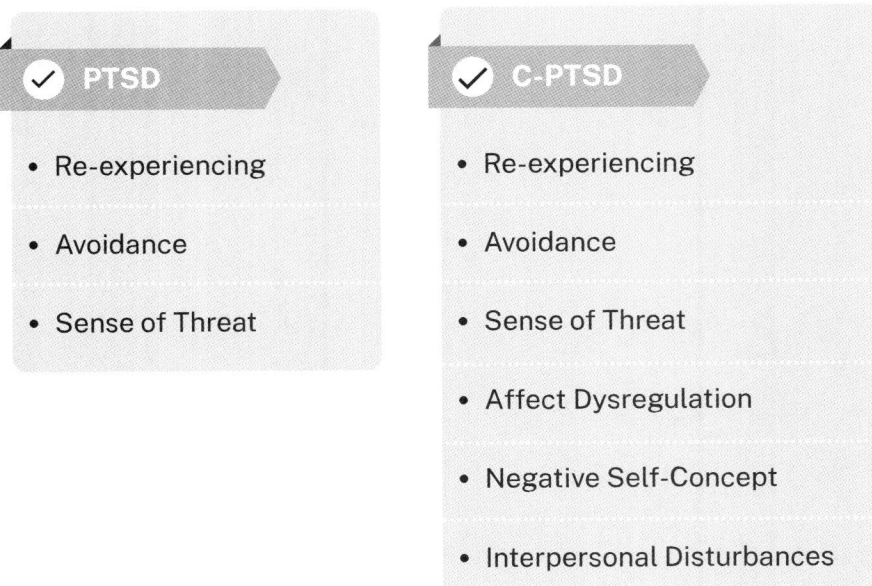

PTSD and C-PTSD Symptoms

As a general overview, PTSD tends to occur in response to one-time events that have a clear beginning and end, come suddenly and unexpectedly, are not a regular part of everyday life, and are immediately life-threatening. Often referred to as "shock trauma" or "event trauma," PTSD can result from experiences such as motor vehicle accidents, physical or sexual attacks, serious injuries, sudden losses, community violence, terrorism, and natural disasters. PTSD focuses on experiences of terror and threats to survival leading to lack of safety, and symptoms associated with physiological dysregulation.

C-PTSD tends to occur in response to ongoing and repeated relational experiences that have no clear beginning or end, are familiar and persistent, are part of one's everyday life, and are not necessarily life-threatening. While there has been a movement for a developmental trauma disorder for children experiencing relational trauma, at this point, both childhood and adult relationally based trauma are categorized within the C-PTSD diagnosis.

C-PTSD can result from many interpersonal experiences children live with (outlined earlier in the ACEs section) such as experiencing ongoing physical, emotional, or sexual abuse, suffering from neglect, witnessing domestic violence, and losing a parent. Additionally, C-PTSD can result from interpersonal experiences adults face such as domestic violence, dislocation, trafficking, enslavement, torture, and other forms of loss of autonomy. C-PTSD focuses on experiences of shame and harm to the Self leading to lack of inner security, and symptoms associated with psychobiological disorganization and relational distress.

**EXERCISES**

**PERSONAL**

# Using the three categories of C-PTSD to reflect on your personal experience

1.  How have adverse childhood experiences led to difficulties in feeling and regulating your emotions in your present life?

2.  How have adverse childhood experiences led to a negative sense of Self in your present life?

3.  How have adverse childhood experiences led to relational difficulties in your present life?

**THERAPIST-ORIENTED**

# Using the three categories of C-PTSD to reflect with a client

1.  Explore with them how the impact of adverse childhood experiences may have led to difficulties in feeling and regulating their emotions in their present life.

2.  Inquire into how adverse childhood experiences may have led to a negative sense of Self in their present life.

3.  Ask them how adverse childhood experiences may have led to relational difficulties in their present life.

# POST-TRAUMATIC GROWTH

*Personal transformation
through healing*

**Post-traumatic growth can be** understood as an opportunity for transformation through the healing of trauma. It is often associated with resiliency, as in the ability to bounce back after life challenges. The five areas of change that post-traumatic growth research generally focuses on are *greater appreciation of life, closer relationships with others, increased personal strength, new possibilities in life,* and *spiritual development.*

We want to better understand the conditions that support humans to experience positive change in response to adversity. Many clients enter into therapy simply seeking symptom reduction, but given the right therapeutic conditions, they can experience new ways of relating to the themselves and new personal capacities and possibilities for their life. NARM offers the relational conditions that optimally support a client's recovery toward personal and relational health. Using their own internal states to inform relational skills, a therapist can promote transformative opportunities for relational healing. The *R* in *NARM* stands for the relational orientation, as outlined in the NARM Relational Model (see p. 83).

Meaningful growth occurs within a human-to-human relational context—whether a child and parent, intimate partners, or therapist and client. The intersubjective process of therapy orients around the therapist's experience as a human being in authentic connection with their client. When we can stay authentically connected with Self and others—no longer stuck in early adaptive survival strategies—humans can experience deep states of connection, belonging, and aliveness.

We use the NARM Personality Spectrum (see p. 127) to assess ten psychobiological traits that determine a client's present capacity and help us assess their movement toward post-traumatic growth. As clients develop greater capacity in these areas, they begin to experience themselves and the world differently, generally with an increased sense of hope, trust, confidence, compassion, gratitude, joy, and love.

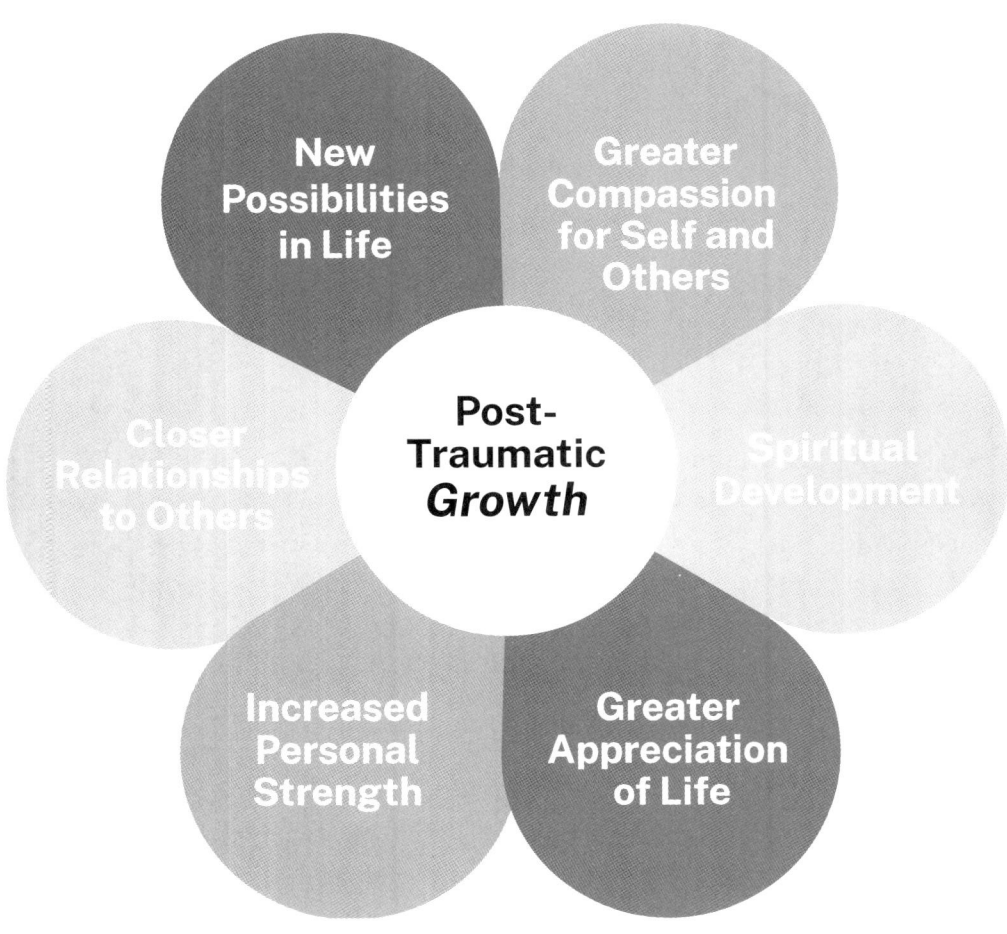

Key aspects of post-traumatic growth

**EXERCISES**

**PERSONAL**

# Reflecting on your own experience with post-traumatic growth

1.   Reflect on a time when you were able to experience significant growth after addressing a traumatic situation.

2.   How did that experience strengthen you?

3.   How is it for you to acknowledge and feel into your resilience and growth?

**THERAPIST-ORIENTED**
# Reflecting with a client

1.   Ask about a time that they were able to experience significant growth after addressing a traumatic situation.

2.   Inquire how that experience strengthened them.

3.   Reflect on how it is to acknowledge and feel into their resilience and growth.

# ADAPTIVE SURVIVAL STYLES

*Reactions to environmental failure and developmental trauma*

**To manage adverse childhood experiences**, children learn to adapt to ensure their survival. We refer to these adaptations as *adaptive survival styles*, which describe personality patterns that coalesce developmentally around emotional and nervous system dysregulation, and faulty beliefs a child uses to construct their early reality. Adaptive survival styles present as psychobiological strategies of disconnection the child adopts to adapt to environmental failure, in a desperate attempt to get love and feel loved. This process leads to distortions in a child's sense of Self, manifesting as patterns of self-shame, self-rejection, and self-hatred that a child carries into adulthood.

These psychobiological adaptations are a child's attempt to protect against relational loss by disconnecting from their core needs and feelings. In the face of attachment and environmental failure, the child learns to foreclose their authentic Self to protect against attachment loss. It leaves children, and later adults, in an impossible bind, what we call in NARM a core dilemma: *"I can either be my authentic Self or have love in my life—but not both."* For a child, the adaptive survival styles are ways to resolve this impossible bind between that which is real within (authentic Self) and that which they have to do in order to survive (adaptive Self).

Children develop adaptive survival styles in response to their environment failing to meet their core needs at critical stages of development. The psychobiological adaptations originate as strategies of disconnecting from, and eventually rejecting, the developmental needs that are going unmet by the adults in their early life. Experiencing the loss of environmental support is devastating to a child and their development. The adaptive survival styles are an attempt to compensate for this early failure and loss but lead to significant psychobiological consequences, shaping the way children, and later as adults, organize, filter, and respond to their life experience. In other words, what was once life saving for a child ends up disrupting their personality development, leading to difficulties in multiple areas of their adult life.

The five adaptive survival styles are named after the core need at each developmental stage: **Connection**, **Attunement**, **Trust**, **Autonomy**, and **Love-Sexuality**. While they are developmentally sequential, individuals may identify with just one, several, or all of these adaptive survival patterns.

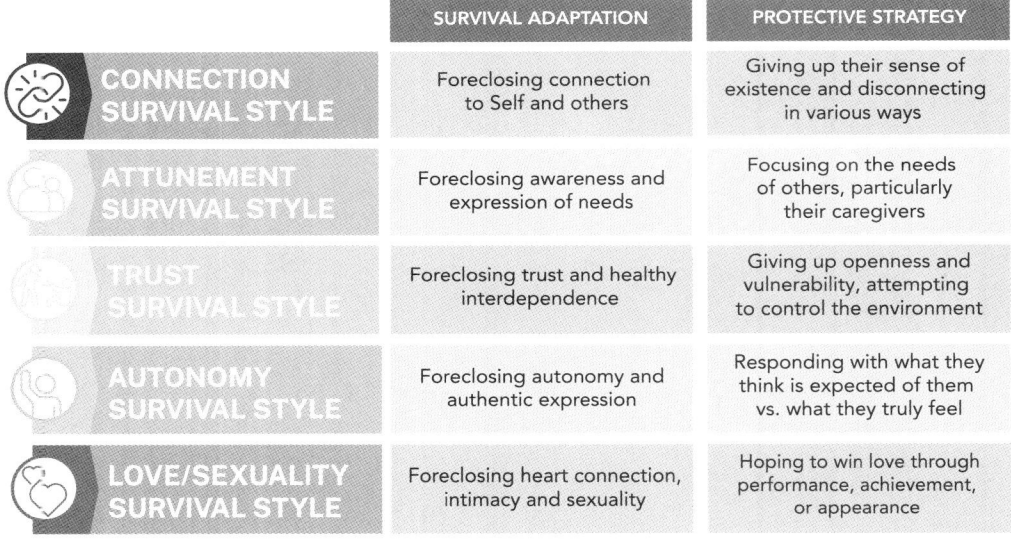

|  | SURVIVAL ADAPTATION | PROTECTIVE STRATEGY |
| --- | --- | --- |
| **CONNECTION SURVIVAL STYLE** | Foreclosing connection to Self and others | Giving up their sense of existence and disconnecting in various ways |
| **ATTUNEMENT SURVIVAL STYLE** | Foreclosing awareness and expression of needs | Focusing on the needs of others, particularly their caregivers |
| **TRUST SURVIVAL STYLE** | Foreclosing trust and healthy interdependence | Giving up openness and vulnerability, attempting to control the environment |
| **AUTONOMY SURVIVAL STYLE** | Foreclosing autonomy and authentic expression | Responding with what they think is expected of them vs. what they truly feel |
| **LOVE/SEXUALITY SURVIVAL STYLE** | Foreclosing heart connection, intimacy and sexuality | Hoping to win love through performance, achievement, or appearance |

The five survival styles and their adaptations

Although they help a young child survive the immediate failures in their early environment, the adaptive styles create an insecure foundation for a child's development and generate varying levels of disorganization of the Self. The childhood strategies outlive their survival necessity and manifest in adult life as the three symptom categories of C-PTSD:

affect dysregulation, negative self-concept, and interpersonal disturbances. Additionally, adaptive survival strategies are the foundation for multiple psychobiological difficulties such as dissociation, depression, anxiety, eating disorders, sleep disorders, sexual disorders, substance abuse disorders, and personality disorders.

We recognize that a client's adaptations are what link their past to their present; the past lives in the present through the adaptive survival styles. The NARM framework emphasizes that the adaptations we carry forward are as important as the original trauma itself. This becomes important clinically as many clients do not remember their early trauma but are presently experiencing self-defeating strategies and debilitating symptoms that may be associated with unresolved adaptive survival responses. The NARM clinical approach is not dependent on a client remembering their early experiences; instead it works directly with their adaptive survival patterns, and the associated strategies and symptoms that are manifesting in the present, to resolve the impact of their early trauma.

Although an understanding of the function and impact of adaptive survival styles is helpful in assessing and treating clients, our primary focus is not on figuring out what specific adaptive survival style our clients used. We have a saying in NARM: *We do not work with survival styles, we work with humans who identify with survival styles.* We recognize that most humans can relate to all the different survival themes to some extent. With our clients, we are exploring how adaptive survival patterns are expressed moment by moment in the relational process. We use this model as a phenomenological framework for helping us understand the inner landscape of each client, and for how we can shape our clinical interventions to best support each unique client.

**PERSONAL**

# Reflecting on your own experience with adapting to environmental failures

1.   What did you have to do in order to adapt to the challenges in your early life?

2.   How have you carried forward your early adaptations into adulthood in relation to your emotions, sense of Self, and relationships?

3.   In what ways do you feel less constrained by these early adaptations in your present life?

**THERAPIST-ORIENTED**

# Reflecting with a client on their experience with adapting to environmental failures

1.  Ask them about what they had to do in order to adapt to the challenges in their early life.

2.  Reflect with them about how they have carried forward their early adaptations into adulthood in relation to their emotions, sense of Self, and relationships.

3.  Inquire into the ways they feel less constrained by these early adaptations in their present life.

# Connection Survival Style

## When Self and others are a threat

What happens when an infant does not feel safe coming into this world? If there's not a welcoming, supportive, and secure holding environment? If there's active abuse, neglect, and other forms of environmental failure? A young child who feels unsafe, unwelcome, and alone in the world, with no possibility for connection, must learn to adapt to the lack of connection, or die.

The desire for connection is hardwired in all of us—connection to ourselves, to others, and to the world. When a young child grows up in a secure and supportive environment, they develop the capacity for connection on all levels of their experience. When a young child does not grow up in a secure and supporting environment, or they face overwhelming trauma at such a young age, they do not develop the full capacity for connection. These children learn to fear connection due to the lack of safety and risk of threat associated with connecting to themselves, others, or the world. Tragically, these children develop significant lifelong challenges around connection, as reflected in their core dilemma: *I need connection, but it doesn't feel safe to connect.*

The desire for and fear of connection becomes an organizing theme for the developing child and leads to adaptive survival strategies of disconnecting from their body, their emotions, their thoughts, their relationships, and their sense of Self, in order to protect themselves from their early trauma. As a way of managing their pain and suffering around such early, profound disconnection, children learn to rely on two main coping strategies: *intellectualizing* and *spiritualizing*. The intellectualizing strategies involve a person disconnecting from themselves by relying on the mental realm, valuing thoughts and logic over feelings and emotions. The spiritualizing strategies involve a person disconnecting from their body, living in the energetic field, and valuing spiritual experience over an embodied, relational one.

Although initially protective, ongoing disconnection from oneself and others leads to profound self-disorganization and difficulties in life. Specifically, clients identified with Connection survival style often feel terrified, isolated, withdrawn, on the outside looking in, powerless, overwhelmed, highly sensitive, dissociated, self-shaming, and self-hating. These areas of distress are what bring these clients into therapy.

Clients identified with the Connection survival style can struggle in therapy due to their challenges with connecting to their body, feelings, and social engagement. Their coping mechanisms include avoidance, shutdown, dissociation, and fragmentation. They often keep things abstract, logical, or spiritualized, and can feel easily overwhelmed, even just by being in the presence of another person. Many therapists find these clients challenging because it's difficult for them to stay present and connect to themselves, often being unable to identify what they're feeling inside or wanting from therapy. Therapists may notice unique countertransference reactions to these clients, for example bemoaning how a client is "all in their head" or "spiritually bypassing."

At the same time, these individuals possess unique strengths and resources, especially as they resolve the core dilemma around connection. They can be highly intelligent, complex and creative thinkers, with rich imaginations, and the ability to think nonlinearly, multidimensionally, and metaphysically. They can also be energetically sensitive, perceptive, intuitive, and spiritually attuned. Due to their deep desire for connection, they may experience great appreciation for the moments of authentic connection they find in life, and especially with other humans, including with their therapist.

## EXERCISES

### PERSONAL
## Reflecting on your relationship to the Connection Survival Style

1. Have you experienced any significant difficulties connecting to yourself or other people?

2. Do you identify with intellectualizing and/or spiritualizing strategies when you experience difficulties in your life?

3.   Reflect on a time when you felt deeply connected—to yourself, to another person, to a pet, to nature, to God. What's it like to reflect on this now?

**THERAPIST-ORIENTED**

# Reflecting with a client who may identify with Connection Survival Style

1.   Ask the client if they have experienced any significant difficulties in connecting to themself or other people.

2.   Ask them if they identify with intellectualizing and/or spiritualizing strategies when they experience difficulties in their life.

3.   Reflect with them on a time when they felt deeply connected—to themself, to another person, to a pet, to nature, to God.

**THERAPIST-ORIENTED**

# Reflecting on a client who may identify with Connection Survival Style

Think about a client who might fit the description of the Connection survival style, and fill in these different aspects to get a sense of how this adaptive survival pattern may impact them in their life and in therapy. Then reflect on how this information can inform and shape your clinical interventions with this client.

- What they most want for themselves in therapy:

- Symptoms they present with:

- Coping strategies/behaviors:

- Strengths and resources:

- What seems to help them in therapy:

- Where you get stuck with them in therapy:

- Your countertransference feelings/reactions:

# Attunement Survival Style

## When needs are a threat

What happens when a very young child experiences ongoing misattunement from their early environment to their basic relational and nurturing needs? If they feel that having and expressing needs are threatening to their attachment figures? When a child becomes afraid of having needs and helpless around the expression of their needs, they face a core dilemma around attunement: *I need attunement, but it doesn't feel safe to have or express my needs.*

Children with ambivalence around having and expressing needs develop survival strategies centered around minimizing and shutting down core needs. Some children learn to not reach out directly and limit their needs to only the minimum of what the environment provides for them; these children are figuratively, and at times literally, waiting for scraps to fall off the table. Some children, especially as they move into adolescence and adulthood, begin suppressing emotions associated with needing; they use food, substances, and other behavioral patterns to distract from need fulfillment. As adults, many people choose professions or relationships where they compulsively give to others what they in fact need for themselves. Most of these people experience guilt and shame associated with needs, including understanding when their needs are met. They often feel that they don't deserve to have their needs met. This leads to symptoms of helplessness, resignation, depression, and despair. These areas of distress are what bring these clients into therapy.

As a way of managing their pain and suffering around misattunement, children learn to rely on two main coping strategies: *inhibited* and *unsatisfied.* With inhibited strategies, a person lacks entitlement around having their needs met, sometimes even takes pride in not having needs, and becomes focused on meeting other people's needs. Using unsatisfied strategies, a person expects others to meet their needs, often in entitled and demanding ways, and when they do get their needs met, they have the feeling that it's never enough, leaving them wanting more.

Clients identified with the Attunement survival style may show up in therapy having difficulty clearly stating what they want from treatment, demonstrating difficulty in knowing and expressing their needs even in therapy. Some clients may use therapy to focus on how they can better meet other people's needs, including the therapist. Other clients may compulsively seek comfort and reassurance from the therapist. Even though the client may not clearly ask for a specific kind of support, they may directly or indirectly express dissatisfaction with their therapist for not meeting their needs.

At the same time these individuals possess unique strengths and resources, especially as they resolve the core dilemma around attunement. They can be emotionally intelligent, perceptive, and compassionate. Oriented toward care, they can be extremely generous and nurturing. Due to their desire for attunement, they may become extremely responsive at identifying and attending to needs in the present moment. They often experience pleasure through helping others, nurturing others, and making sure that others feel happy and fulfilled.

## EXERCISES

### PERSONAL
## Reflecting on your relationship to the Attunement Survival Style

1.  Have you noticed any internal resistance to reflecting on your needs?

2.  Do you feel a lack of sense of entitlement to express your needs, or do you get the feedback that you are sometimes overly demanding?

3.   What's it like to recall a time when you expressed your needs, and someone responded positively?

# Reflecting with a client who may identify with Attunement Survival Style

1.   Ask them if they have noticed any internal resistance to reflecting on their needs.

2.   Inquire if they feel a lack of entitlement to express their needs, or do they get the feedback that they are sometimes overly demanding.

3.  Ask about a time when they expressed their needs, and someone responded positively.

**THERAPIST-ORIENTED**

# Reflecting on a client who may identify with Attunement Survival Style

Reflect on a client who might fit the description of the Attunement survival style, and fill in these different aspects to get a sense of how this adaptive survival pattern may impact them in their life and in therapy. Then reflect on how this information can inform and shape your clinical interventions with this client.

- What they most want for themselves in therapy:

- Symptoms they present with:

- Coping strategies/behaviors:

- Strengths and resources:

- What seems to help them in therapy:

- Where you get stuck with them in therapy:

- Your countertransference feelings/reactions:

# Trust Survival Style

## When dependence is a threat

What happens when a child experiences an ongoing sense of helplessness and power-lessness? If they feel there are no adults they can depend on? When a child feels afraid, betrayed, out of control, and that their environment will not keep them safe, they face a core dilemma around trust: *I need to trust and depend on others, but it doesn't feel safe to trust and depend on others.*

The ambivalence around trust and dependence leads to adaptive survival strategies organized around control and power. When a child grows up in an atmosphere of abuse, has no dependable caregivers, and is forced to grow up before they're ready, they experience fear and terror. Similarly, if a child is rewarded for giving up their authenticity in order to be what the caregiver wants them to be, they experience a deep betrayal. They lose a sense of control and power in their early environment and relationships, and carry the sense of vulnerability and powerlessness forward in their lives.

To protect themselves from an intolerable sense of vulnerability, they rely on strategies of manipulating, competing, intimidating, seducing, gaslighting, and attacking. They focus on boosting themselves in various ways, trying to compensate for how powerless they feel by being big, strong, smart, successful, special, and impervious to vulnerability and failure. There is a wide spectrum of how this is expressed, from micromanagers and control freaks to malignant narcissists and psychopaths.

As a way of managing their pain and suffering around breaches of trust and dependence—and the extreme vulnerability and powerlessness this engenders—children learn to rely on two main coping strategies: *overpowering* and *seductive.* Overpowering involves a person asserting control over others by becoming physically, behaviorally, financially, or spiritually "one-up," evoking intimidation, fear, and obedience from others. Seductive strategies involve a person manipulating and seducing others in order to gain their trust and confidence, which renders other people powerless, dependent, and no longer a threat.

Clients identified with the Trust survival style don't generally come to therapy voluntarily but may be forced into therapy by their spouses, employers, or the criminal justice system. When these clients do come in voluntarily, it's often after a life collapse—for example, a divorce, loss of job, bankruptcy, or hitting "rock bottom" in their addiction. As clients, they struggle with the vulnerability and power dynamics they experience in therapy. Wanting to remain in control, they may be very sensitive to feedback or have other relational challenges based in distrust of therapy or the therapist, and may leave therapy if they begin to feel threatened.

At the same time, these individuals possess unique strengths and resources, especially as they resolve the core dilemma around trust. They can be focused, decisive, effective, and self-reliant. They can be natural leaders, empowering and inspiring others based on their confidence and charisma. These individuals may show up fully for life experience, with the courage to take charge, take risks, and break new ground. They can be bold and adventurous, thriving on adventure, challenge, and competition.

## EXERCISES

### PERSONAL
## Reflecting on your relationship to the Trust Survival Style

1.  Have you noticed any internal resistance to trusting and depending on others?

2.  Do you notice yourself trying to get your way in relationships and situations by overpowering or manipulating people?

3. Can you recall a positive experience when you were able to trust and depend on someone?

**THERAPIST-ORIENTED**

# Reflecting with a client who may identify with Trust Survival Style

1. Ask them if they have noticed any internal resistance to trusting and depending on others.

2. Inquire if they notice themself trying to get their way in relationships and situations by overpowering or manipulating people.

**3.**   Ask them to share a positive experience when they were able to trust and depend on someone.

**THERAPIST-ORIENTED**

# Reflecting on a client who may identify with Trust Survival Style

Think about a client who might fit the description of the Trust survival style, and fill in these different aspects to get a sense of how this adaptive survival pattern may impact them in their life and in therapy. Then reflect on how this information can inform and shape your clinical interventions with this client.

- What they most want for themselves in therapy:

- Symptoms they present with:

- Coping strategies/behaviors:

- Strengths and resources:

- What seems to help them in therapy:

- Where you get stuck with them in therapy:

- Your countertransference feelings/reactions:

# Autonomy Survival Style

## When independence is a threat

What happens when a child cannot experience their autonomy? If they aren't supported to learn how to act independently and make their own choices? When a child's capacity for authenticity and self-determination are consistently thwarted by their environment, they face a core dilemma around autonomy: *I need to experience my independence, but it doesn't feel safe to express my independence openly.*

The ambivalence around autonomy, independence, and self-determination leads to adaptive survival strategies related to internal pressure, which may be perceived as coming from the outside. These individuals fear that people won't like or accept them if they are authentic and self-express. So they become ruled by "shoulds," not trusting their own instincts, and instead act how they think others want them to act, and become who they think they're supposed to be. While they put pressure on themselves to be agreeable, likeable, responsible, trustworthy, and people-pleasing, inside they hold feelings of shame, humiliation, resentment, and simmering rage. These repressed feelings lead to incongruence in communication, ambivalence in making choices, difficulty in setting and maintaining boundaries, and avoiding conflict. This can also lead to self-sabotaging behaviors, such as rumination, procrastination, not leaving unhealthy relationships or situations, and saying yes when they want to say no.

As a way of managing their pain and suffering around not being able to express their autonomy, children learn to rely on two main coping strategies: *submissive* and *rebellious.* Submissive strategies include a person being compliant, pleasing, self-sacrificing, and taking pride in how much they can take on without saying no or expressing their distress directly. Using rebellious strategies, a person projects authority on the outside and then rebels against this perceived authority, which may be expressed directly as defiance, or expressed indirectly through nonaction and passive-aggressive behaviors. Some individuals may even find a secret enjoyment in disappointing people, including their therapist.

Clients identified with the Autonomy survival style may initially feel easy to work with, especially if they present with compliant, people-pleasing strategies, but over time both therapist and client often feel stuck. Due to the client's deep ambivalence, lack of transparency, and fear of saying what's true for them, the client will try and figure out what the therapist expects from them, and then superficially try to give them that, while on a deeper level resenting the therapist's "program" for them. Other times, especially if the client presents with defiant strategies, the client will rebel—either quietly or loudly—against the therapist or any perceived agenda the therapy has for them, blocking any forward movement. Faced with compulsive compliance or defiance, therapists feel at a loss for how to proceed, and often feel defeated with these clients.

At the same time, these individuals possess unique strengths and resources, especially as they resolve the core dilemma around autonomy. They can be mindful and reflective about others with a desire to be loyal friends and colleagues. In their support of others, they can be extremely patient, tolerant, and accepting. These individuals can be grounded and determined advocates, especially in helping others experience greater freedom and justice in their lives. They may have the ability to see all sides of a situation, which makes for good problem-solving and mediation, helping people work through challenging situations.

**EXERCISES**

**PERSONAL**

## Reflecting on your relationship to the Autonomy Survival Style

1.  Have you noticed any internal resistance to standing up for yourself?

2.  Do you tend to be more submissive or rebellious in your responses when someone tells you what to do?

3. Can you recall a time when you stood up for yourself in a relation-ship, and felt good about it?

**THERAPIST-ORIENTED**

# Reflecting with a client who may identify with Autonomy Survival Style

1. Ask them if they have noticed any internal resistance to standing up for themselves.

2. Inquire if they tend to be more submissive or rebellious in their responses when someone tells them what to do.

3.   Ask them about a time when they stood up for themselves in a relationship, and felt good about it.

**THERAPIST-ORIENTED**

# Reflecting on a client who may identify with Autonomy Survival Style

Reflect on a client who might fit the description of the Autonomy survival style, and fill in these different aspects to get a sense of how this adaptive survival pattern may impact them in their life and in therapy. Then reflect on how this information can inform and shape your clinical interventions with this client.

• What they most want for themselves in therapy:

• Symptoms they present with:

• Coping strategies/behaviors:

• Strengths and resources:

• What seems to help them in therapy:

• Where you get stuck with them in therapy:

• Your countertransference feelings/reactions:

# Love-Sexuality Survival Style

## When love and intimacy are threats

What happens when a child reaches out to the world with love and experiences heartbreak? If their tenderness, affection, and openheartedness are rejected? When a child's capacity for bringing their heart into relationships is rejected, they are faced with a core dilemma around love: *I want to express and receive love, but it doesn't feel safe to do either one.*

The ambivalence around love, often in combination with shame around their body and sexuality, leads to adaptive survival strategies related to self-control, rigidity, and perfectionism. In an obsessive pursuit to not experience failure and rejection, these individuals can be extremely driven, focusing on performance, achievement, and admiration. They may emphasize doing it correctly, have a strict moral code for themselves and others, and believe that mistakes must be punished. Valuing looks and status, they can be highly critical of themselves and others, rooted in a desire to be seen as exceptional. They may believe that being loved is based on how they look and how they perform. Relationally, they often reject others before the possibility of being rejected, leading to difficulties in relationships and intimacy.

As a way of managing their pain around living in connection with their tender loving feelings, children learn to rely on two main coping strategies, particularly observable in adult relationships: *romantic* and *sexual.* Using romantic strategies, a person may romanticize love and marriage but have difficulty maintaining sexual intimacy. With sexual strategies, a person uses sexual relationships as a means to bolster self-esteem but is emotionally distant, blocking the possibility of heart connection.

Clients identified with the Love-Sexuality survival style may relate to therapy as yet another aspect of their ongoing self-improvement focus. Engaging in therapy through their high, often unrealistic expectations, coupled with intense self-criticism, they often doubt their ability to find a suitable partner and be successful in love relationships. Their desire to be seen as perfect creates challenges to sharing their vulnerability, lest they appear inadequate or flawed. Showing flaws is experienced as being unlovable. Therapists may feel challenged by a lack of depth in clients who are desperately attempting to keep it together in fear of exposing their core needs around loving and being loved.

At the same time, these individuals possess unique strengths and resources, especially as they resolve the core dilemma around loving. They tend to be committed to excellence in all their pursuits and take pleasure in a job well done. They may be able to appreciate the successes and pleasures in life. They often have a strong, focused attention, which gives them the ability to be responsible, thorough, precise, and follow through with agreements and projects. With their drive for achievement, they can be extremely competent and excellent performers in many areas.

**EXERCISES**

**PERSONAL**

# Reflecting on your relationship to the Love-Sexuality Survival Style

1. Have you noticed any internal resistance to opening your heart in intimate relationships?

2. Do you tend to have difficulties opening your heart or sharing your sexuality in close relationships?

3. Can you recall a time when you opened your heart in an intimate relationship, and it was reciprocated by another person?

**THERAPIST-ORIENTED**

# Reflecting with a client who may identify with Love-Sexuality Survival Style

1. Ask them if they have noticed any internal resistance to opening their heart in intimate relationships.

2. Inquire if they tend to have difficulties opening their heart or sharing their sexuality when in close relationships.

3. Ask them about a time when they opened their heart in an intimate relationship, and it was reciprocated by another person.

**THERAPIST-ORIENTED**

# Reflecting on a client who may identify with Love-Sexuality Survival Style

Think about a client who might fit the description of the Love-Sexuality survival style, and fill in these different aspects to get a sense of how this adaptive survival pattern may impact them in their life and in therapy. Then reflect on how this information can inform and shape your clinical interventions with this client.

- What they most want for themselves in therapy:

- Symptoms they present with:

- Coping strategies/behaviors:

- Strengths and resources:

- What seems to help them in therapy:

- Where you get stuck with them in therapy:

- Your countertransference feelings/reactions:

# Resolution of Adaptive Survival Styles

## Freedom from developmental trauma patterns

Understanding adaptive survival styles helps NARM therapists organize our therapeutic approach. Although a client's history, memory, and narratives are important, these areas are not the primary focus of NARM. We do not rely on childhood history to grasp the complex nature of our clients' issues, nor do we focus on the specific traumas they experienced. We focus on how clients have learned to adapt to these traumatic experiences and how unresolved developmental themes express themselves in clients' present lives.

The survival styles provide a valuable framework to help us understand how clients are organizing their internal experience and relating to their external experience—how they form their sense of Self. Clients who have experienced early trauma develop various cognitive, emotional, behavioral, and relational strategies in reaction to the unresolved, impossible binds around the needs for *connection, attunement, trust, autonomy,* and *love-sexuality*.

As a reminder, we do not use these survival styles to classify and categorize our clients. We use this framework to help identify developmental themes that are driving so much of the present suffering that our clients experience. We explore how survival patterns are expressed moment by moment in the clinical process. We use this phenomenological framework to better understand how our clients shape their inner worlds, and to guide the interventions we use with them.

However, working with these deeper psychobiological layers of personality can feel threatening to clients, at least initially. As a person shifts old patterns, they begin to challenge what they have taken to be their identity and who they believe themselves to be. When clients begin to experience this disidentification process and realize the limitations of who they have understood themselves to be, change can happen more quickly than they may anticipate.

Once clients start to feel their increasing psychobiological capacity, they appreciate the transformative nature of this work. A concept similar to "window of tolerance" or "range of resiliency," psychobiological capacity represents movement toward greater organization within the Self. As these unresolved developmental themes are transformed into core capacities for well-being, clients embody a sense of increasing internal freedom and begin experiencing themselves, their relationships, their history, and their life in a new way.

| CORE CAPACITIES ESSENTIAL FOR WELL-BEING |
| --- |

**CONNECTION SURVIVAL STYLE**
Capacity to be in touch with our body and emotions
Capacity to be in connection with others

**ATTUNEMENT SURVIVAL STYLE**
Capacity to attune to our needs and emotions
Capacity to recognize, reach out for, and take in nourishment

**TRUST SURVIVAL STYLE**
Capacity to have healthy dependence and interdependence

**AUTONOMY SURVIVAL STYLE**
Capacity to set boundaries and say no
Capacity to speak our mind without fear, guilt, or shame

**LOVE/SEXUALITY SURVIVAL STYLE**
Capacity to live with an open heart
Capacity to integrate loving relationship and sexuality

The five survival styles and their core capacities for well-being

**EXERCISES**

**PERSONAL**

# Reflecting on your relationship to the adaptive survival styles

1.   Which of the adaptive survival styles do you most relate to?

2. How have these survival patterns created difficulties for you?

3. How has the personal work you've done in your life changed one or more of these adaptive survival styles?

**THERAPIST-ORIENTED**

## Reflecting with a client who may identify with adaptive survival styles

1. Ask them which of the adaptive survival styles they most relate to.

2. Inquire into how these adaptive survival patterns have created difficulties for them in their adult life.

3. Reflect on how their healing work has changed one or more of these adaptive survival styles.

# NARM FOUR PILLARS

——

*Relational skills for post-traumatic growth*

**The NARM Four Pillars** are the therapeutic skills that support a client's healing and post-traumatic growth. The Four Pillars provide a clinical approach for addressing how adaptive survival patterns are impacting a client in their present life and for supporting new ways they can relate to themselves. Designed as a relational process to promote increasing intersubjectivity, the Four Pillars help bring a client more into the here and now of their present life and thereby strengthen their capacity for connection to their inner world and to other people—and in so doing, resolve the wounds of developmental trauma.

Although we are presenting the Four Pillars sequentially, the NARM approach does not follow a strict protocol and we do not consider it a manualized therapy. We meet the client where they are and thus apply the Four Pillars fluidly in relationship. Over time, therapists learn various ways to apply these interventions and skills in relation to the unique client sitting in front of them.

The following pages provide guidance on how to apply the NARM Four Pillars:

**Pillar 1: Clarifying the Therapeutic Contract** supports the client to set the intention for their healing process. By inviting the client to connect to what they most want for

# NARM FOUR PILLARS

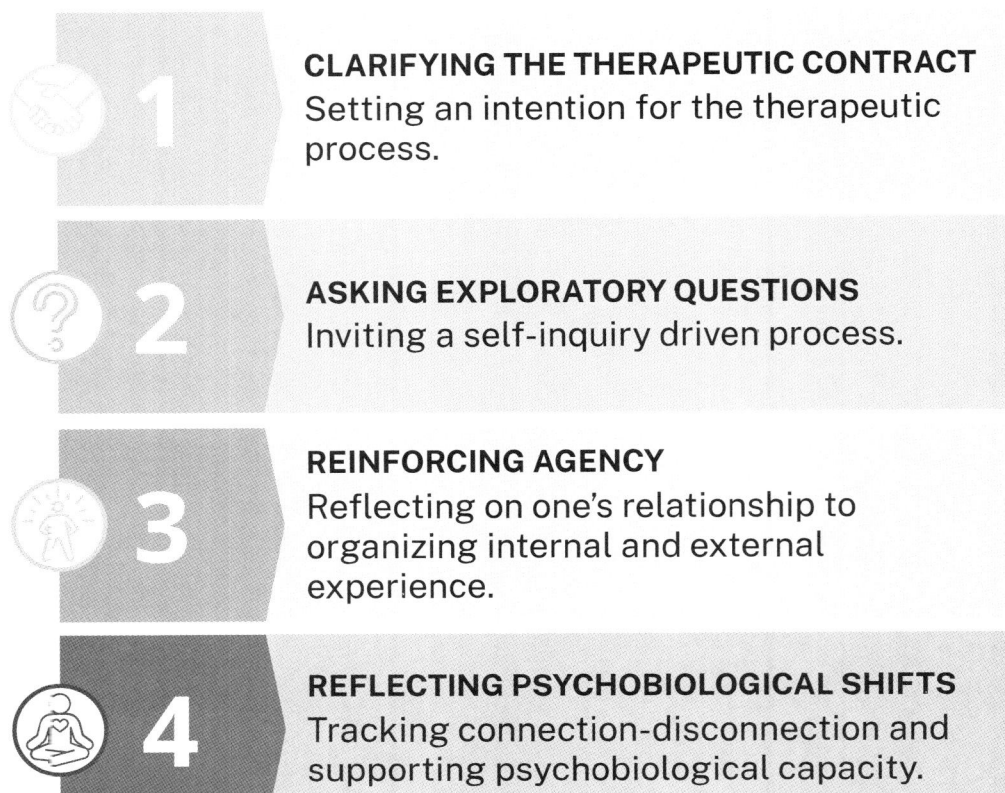

**1**   **CLARIFYING THE THERAPEUTIC CONTRACT**
Setting an intention for the therapeutic process.

**2**   **ASKING EXPLORATORY QUESTIONS**
Inviting a self-inquiry driven process.

**3**   **REINFORCING AGENCY**
Reflecting on one's relationship to organizing internal and external experience.

**4**   **REFLECTING PSYCHOBIOLOGICAL SHIFTS**
Tracking connection-disconnection and supporting psychobiological capacity.

The Four Pillars

themself from their work with us, therapists can begin to support an agency-based process focused on exploration, which allows for a collaborative process built upon client intent and relational consent.

**Pillar 2: Asking Exploratory Questions** drives how therapists engage with their clients. This inquiry-based process supports therapists and invites clients to reflect on and gather information about their subjective experience. Specifically, therapists bring curiosity to the internal obstacles that are in the client's way of getting what they most want for themself.

**Pillar 3: Reinforcing Agency** supports a client's developing capacity for awareness of the active role they play in their own emotional and relational difficulties, specifically how they are organizing their internal experience in ways that reinforce old trauma patterns. This agency-oriented process supports the possibility that clients can learn new, more life-affirming ways of relating to themselves and others.

**Pillar 4: Reflecting Psychobiological Shifts** provides opportunities for clients to notice changes on all levels of their internal experience—including the physical, emotional, cognitive, relational, and spiritual. As clients develop greater awareness for tracking the psychobiological patterns of connection and disconnection, therapists help clients anchor shifts toward increasing connection. This process supports clients to connect to and embody changes in their internal experience as they begin relating to themselves in new ways—which reinforces an internal process of integration, organization, and transformation.

## EXERCISES

### PERSONAL
## Using the Four Pillars to reflect on your relationship to a theme or symptom in your life that you'd like to be different

1.  What is it that you're really wanting for yourself? How would you imagine your life might be different?

2.  What internal obstacles to change might be in your way?

3.   What role might you be playing in this? How might you be relating to yourself in ways that reinforce the internal obstacles?

4.   What do you notice internally as you imagine this different life? What are you experiencing physically and emotionally?

**THERAPIST-ORIENTED**

# Using the Four Pillars to reflect with a client on their relationship to a theme or symptom in their life that they'd like to be different

1.   Ask them what it is that they really want for themself—how they imagine their life might be different.

2.  Inquire into what is in their way of change—what internal obstacles might be in their way.

3.  Explore with them what role they might be playing in this—how might they be relating to themself in ways that reinforce the internal obstacles.

4.  Reflect with them on what they notice internally as they imagine this different life—what they are experiencing physically and emotionally.

# PILLAR 1:
# Clarifying the Therapeutic Contract

Pillar 1 helps us know what it is that our client wants from the therapeutic process. Additionally, it helps us use the client's intention to establish an organizing thread for each session, and in the ongoing therapy process.

Pillar 1 is about creating a collaborative working relationship where the client provides the fuel for the therapeutic change. From the outset of the therapeutic process, and at the beginning of each therapy session, we establish relational consent by inquiring around the client's desire for themselves. We use the word *contract* in the spirit of its original meaning, "to draw together," in which a client's intention for themselves draws together the therapist's attention with the client's inner world. The therapist focuses their curiosity and attention on what the client truly wants for themselves, which invites an exploration into the obstacles that may be in the way of what they most want. This provides clarity and direction in moving forward in therapy.

How do we know when we have clarified a solid therapeutic contract? Sometimes the client will directly report this to us—for example, "Yes, this is exactly what I'm wanting!" And sometimes it is more subtle, felt as an energetic and somatic sensation that things are coming together. As a client clarifies their intention, we may observe in our clients, or feel in the resonance between us and our clients:

- More clarity
- More simplicity
- More connected
- More attuned

- More feeling
- More presence
- A settling into their body (some NARM therapists refer to this as "kerplunk")

Many clients initially may say "I don't know" or even tell us that they don't like this question. As children, most clients did not experience others as having interest and patience with their internal world, so a therapist providing this interest and patience can begin to support a new way that the client can relate to themselves and the relationship. As therapy progresses, we often find that clients internalize this process and come into therapy ready to share with us what they want out of therapy—demonstrating that they're learning how to relate to themself with more interest, patience, and self-support.

Pillar 1 leads to a collaborative working agreement that supports a client's sense of agency and ownership in the change process. There are three steps to this clinical process, reflected in the acronym *AIM*:

**1.** *Ask* their intention for change

**2.** *Impact* of their intention

**3.** *Mirror* intention to receive consent for further exploration

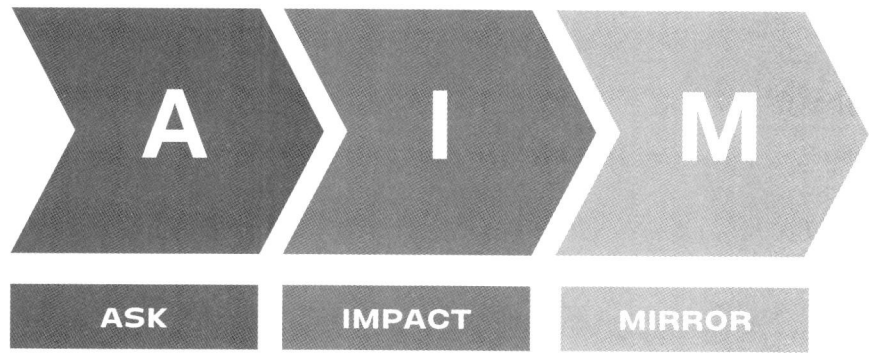

**AIM process of Pillar 1**

There are various ways we might phrase these three clinical steps, but here are a few examples:

**1.** *Asking* client to reflect on their intention for therapy:

*What would you like for yourself today?*

*What would you hope to get out of our time together today?*

**2.** Inquiring how their intention might *impact* them:

*If you're able to get this for yourself, what might you hope for?*

*What would be an optimal outcome, even if it's not realistic?*

**3.** Clarifying and *mirroring* their intention, and agreeing to explore the obstacles to their intention:

*I would be happy to explore what's in your way of. . . .*

*How does it sound to you for us to explore what's in your way of . . .?*

For example, a client who is feeling anxious and depressed comes into therapy, and the therapist begins by inquiring into what they want out of therapy.

THERAPIST: *What would you like for yourself out of therapy?*

CLIENT: *I don't know. I'm anxious and sad all the time.*

THERAPIST: *If you were able to shift these feelings of anxiousness and sadness, what would you hope for yourself?*

CLIENT: *I wouldn't feel uncomfortable all the time.*

THERAPIST: *And if you didn't feel uncomfortable all the time, what would you hope to experience for yourself?*

CLIENT: *I guess I'd feel more confident.*

THERAPIST: *So if you're able to shift feeling uncomfortable all the time, you'd like to feel more confident?*

CLIENT: *Yes, definitely more confident. And at peace.*

THERAPIST: *I'd be happy to explore what's in the way of you feeling more confident and at peace in your life. How does this sound?*

CLIENT: *Yes, please!*

## Establishing the Therapeutic Contract Might Sound Like:

"What would you like for yourself today?"

"What would you hope to get out of our time together today?"

"What would be the optimal outcome out of therapy, even if it's not realistic?"

"If you were able to feel less angry, how might you hope that would impact your life?"

"If you were able to feel less angry, what might that bring for you?"

"I'm happy to explore what's driving your anger and getting in the way of feeling more peaceful inside."

"I'm happy to explore what's getting in the way of feeling less anxious."

"I'm happy to explore what's getting in the way of you feeling more capacity for confidence."

Example questions and phrases of Pillar 1

When clients are invited to reflect on their desire for change, their intentions become guiding principles for how they want to be in the world. In the example here, the client needs a little support and guidance to clarify what they want out of therapy. Once the client is able to clarify their intention to feel more confident and at peace, the therapist and client can begin exploring the obstacles in the way of actualizing the client's intention. This process sets the stage for reconnecting to one's authentic Self and healing unresolved patterns of complex trauma.

## THERAPEUTIC SHORTCUTS FOR PILLAR 1

- While clients generally come into therapy to change symptoms and behaviors, the focus of Pillar 1 is on the client's desired internal state.

- The client sets their intention for the work: *What is it that the client truly wants for themselves?*

- The client's intention does not have to be realistic; in fact, we may want to invite reflection on their heart's desire or optimal outcome.

- We want to be mindful and remember that it is the client's intention that fuels therapeutic change.

- It is essential that the therapist establishes agreement with the client around their intention before moving forward into deeper exploration.

- Contracting sets the collaborative tone of NARM therapy.

- Central to the collaborative nature of Pillar 1 is treating the client like an equal partner in the therapeutic process.

- We're helping the client become their own expert in their internal world.

- For some clients, anything other than symptom relief is difficult to identify—this in itself is diagnostic of their level of internal organization.

- The therapist relates to contracting as an exploration-oriented process, not a goal-oriented process.

- The therapist does not pressure themself or clients to "get a contract" but uses the contracting process for learning about how a client is relating to their present experience.

- Therapy does not start after the contract is established; the contracting process itself is an important element of the healing process.

- It is useful to reflect on the initial contract throughout the session and over the course of therapy.

- Whenever needed, the therapist and client can always recontract during the session.

- While some NARM therapists begin every session using the Pillar 1 AIM process, other NARM therapists might work with a client's intention over a number of sessions.

**EXERCISES**

**PERSONAL**

# Using Pillar 1 to reflect for yourself

1.  Reflect on some capacity that you most want for yourself.

2.  How do you hope your life might be different if you are able to access this capacity?

3.  What do you experience as you reflect on this possibility?

# Using Pillar 1 to reflect with a client

1.   Ask the client to reflect on some capacity that they most want for themselves.

2.   Inquire how they hope their life might be different if they are able to access this capacity.

3.   Inquire about what they experience as they reflect on this possibility.

# PILLAR 2:
## Asking Exploratory Questions

Pillar 2 is an inquiry process that helps a client connect to, experience, and understand their inner world. The questions NARM therapists ask are designed to support clients to learn more about themselves, provide therapists with an opportunity to learn more about their clients, and enhance interpersonal attunement and connection. Ultimately, inquiry is designed to support a client's increasing internal organization (Self-organization).

Many clients have never had anyone truly express interest in and have the capacity to stay present to their inner world. Traditionally, parents, teachers, and even therapists have focused on behaviors, performance, results, and goals. When therapists do this, even with the best intentions, clients can feel misattuned to and profoundly missed. The questions we use are designed for depth—getting underneath the symptoms and behaviors to where the Self lives.

Inquiry itself is a powerful clinical intervention. We ask questions that lead clients into new territory within themselves, giving them an opportunity to challenge and shift old adaptive survival patterns. The questions we use aren't designed to get specific answers. We recognize that every response from a client is the "right" answer, because whatever response they give provides useful information in helping us better understand the client's internal world. So if a client gets confused, angry, sad, or reactive about a question, that response gives us valuable information as to how they are relating to this present experience. These answers may hold clues as to obstacles in the way of what the client says they want from themself (Pillar 1).

As part of our exploratory questions, we are attempting to break down complex elements so that the client truly understands them and can relate to them in a new way. This deconstruction process helps clients untangle aspects of their life experience that often feels messy, confusing, and overwhelming. Relating more directly to specific elements of a complex dynamic helps clients experience greater clarity and capacity to manage their situation.

We use two main interventions to support this deconstruction process: *drilling down* and *deconstruction of experience*. *Drilling down* involves gathering more information on all levels of experience by inviting more clarity or specificity to something that may be unclear, vague, or general. For example, a client who wants to feel more grounded in their life is feeling anxious, upset, and reactive at work. The therapist follows a thread of inquiry by clarifying a client's phrase that is vague.

CLIENT: *I'm just sick of it.*

THERAPIST: *When you say that you are sick of "it," what is the "it" you are sick of?*

CLIENT: *All the crap.*

THERAPIST: *And when you refer to "crap," what do you mean exactly?*

CLIENT: *The way that my boss keeps getting on me but is always nice to my coworkers.*

THERAPIST: *And when you see your boss getting on you but always being nice to your coworkers, what do you make of this experience?*

CLIENT: *That it's happening again. I am always pushed aside, always on the outside looking in.*

THERAPIST: *So it sounds like the "it" you are sick of is being pushed aside and being on the outside looking in?*

CLIENT: *Yes, exactly!*

THERAPIST: *Is this a familiar pattern for you?*

CLIENT: *All my life! It's the source of so much pain.*

In this example, the therapist uses inquiry to peel back the layers of language that initially conceals more than it reveals, until the client is able to name an old, familiar pattern that has caused them "so much pain." Now that this pattern has been clarified, the therapist and client can more directly explore how it is impacting the client's current difficulties at work and getting in their way of feeling more grounded in their life.

*Deconstruction of experience* is addressing a specific situation that reflects the difficulty the client experiences, helping them untangle the various elements of this life experience. For example, a client who feels insecure in their relationship wants to feel more confident. The therapist asks them to choose a recent time in their relationship when they were feeling insecure and a lack of confidence, and then slows down this experience to help unpack this complex dynamic.

THERAPIST: *Do you have an example of a recent time in your relationship when you were feeling insecure and a lack of confidence?*

CLIENT: *The other day I wanted to tell my partner how I was feeling but I got anxious and tongue-tied. I couldn't say what I wanted to say.*

THERAPIST: *So you wanted to tell your partner how you were feeling but you started to feel anxious. Do you have a sense of what you were anxious about in that moment?*

CLIENT: *I don't know. But this happens to me all the time.*

THERAPIST: *OK. But if we just take this specific example, if you told your partner how you were feeling, what do you worry might happen?*

CLIENT: *That she will leave me. But it's really ridiculous that I fear that—I know she loves me. It's embarrassing.*

THERAPIST: *So when you name the fear of your partner leaving you, you tell yourself that it's embarrassing?*

CLIENT: *Yes, I feel like a loser.*

THERAPIST: *So you feel embarrassed, and you feel like a loser?*

CLIENT: *I always attack myself after these experiences. I do feel like a loser and that my partner knows that and she will leave me.*

THERAPIST: *I wonder if your insecurity and lack of confidence might be related to the way you attack yourself and call yourself a loser?*

CLIENT: *I hadn't thought about it like that before, but it makes sense why I'd feel insecure and anxious if I'm always feeling like a loser.*

THERAPIST: *How is it to notice this connection?*

CLIENT: *It actually feels strangely good. If I feel insecure because I am attacking myself, then if I stop attacking myself, I might feel more confident. That's hopeful!*

In this example, the therapist helps the client deconstruct a current situation and is able to uncover an old narrative the client holds about themselves (i.e., "I feel like a loser") that has been a major source of their suffering. As the client unpacks the various elements that lead them to feel insecure and unconfident, they begin to find more hope for changing this pattern.

Ultimately, the intention of exploring internal obstacles through inquiry is to support the possibility of increased connection to the client's authentic Self, providing them with opportunities for shifting old adaptive survival strategies and moving toward healing, change, and growth.

# THERAPEUTIC SHORTCUTS
# FOR PILLAR 2

- Our exploration follows the thread of the session, which is informed by the therapeutic contract (Pillar 1).

- NARM inquiry is driven by deep curiosity about the client's inner world.

- *Drilling down* is simply gathering more information on all levels of experience via inquiring about the details of whatever is being shared or experienced by the client.

- *Deconstruction of experience* invites a client to share a specific experience relating to a larger pattern driving their distress that the therapist helps deconstruct by inquiring into their present-moment somatic, emotional, and cognitive experience of this dynamic.

- Our questions are primarily focused on what's happening in the present moment, in the here and now, because only in the here and now can the connection-disconnection process be observed and reflected.

- Our inquiry focuses on what is surfacing in the therapeutic relationship moment by moment.

- We try to use simple, concise language, as too many words and overly complex thoughts can take clients out of their present experience and keep them stuck in the cognitive realm.

- We focus primarily on process, and secondarily on content.

- We focus on how the client relates to themself and not specifically the narrative they have for themself.

- Our questions lead to a working hypothesis about how our clients are organizing their internal experience.

- Our working hypothesis then informs more nuanced and incisive questions related to how our clients are organizing their internal experience.

- Self-agency is a central aspect of inquiry, as we're helping clients recognize their part in their emotional and relational difficulties.

- All information is valuable information and becomes part of the inquiry.

## Asking Exploratory Questions Might Sound Like:

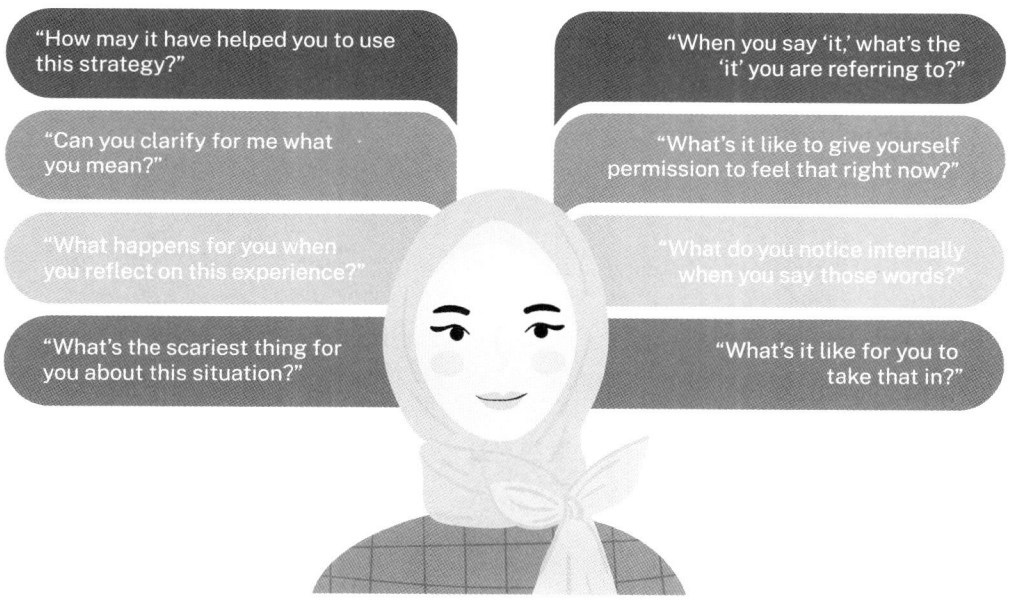

"How may it have helped you to use this strategy?"

"When you say 'it,' what's the 'it' you are referring to?"

"Can you clarify for me what you mean?"

"What's it like to give yourself permission to feel that right now?"

"What happens for you when you reflect on this experience?"

"What do you notice internally when you say those words?"

"What's the scariest thing for you about this situation?"

"What's it like for you to take that in?"

Examples of questions and phrases of Pillar 2

Pillar 2 is about how we invite clients into greater capacity for self-inquiry, self-reflection, and curiosity. Following are some examples of questions we might use with clients—we invite you to be curious about your clients' experience and add more questions you might ask them.

- Can you think of a specific incident when you had this reaction, so we can look at it in greater detail?
- What is the meaning that you took out of that experience about yourself and the world?
- When you say "it," what is the "it" you are referring to?
- What do you mean exactly by that?
- Can you clarify for me what you mean?
- What's the scariest thing for you about this situation?
- How might it have helped you to use this strategy?
- What do you notice internally when you say those words?
- What's it like as you stay present to what you are experiencing internally right now?
- Is there anything else that you can say about this feeling?
- What happens for you when you reflect on this experience?
- What's it like for you when you take that in?
- What's it like to give yourself permission to feel that?
- What are you experiencing overall right now?

Remember, it is not the content of the questions, or getting the "right" questions, that supports the deepening of connection and the possibility of change; *it's in the spirit of inquiry.*

**EXERCISES**

**PERSONAL**

# Using Pillar 2 to reflect for yourself

1. Reflect on a personal obstacle (e.g., fear) in the way of what you're wanting for yourself.

2. Choose a specific example of a situation where you experienced this personal obstacle, and see if you're able to unpack the different aspects of this situation that contributed to your distress.

3. What do you become aware of as you give yourself time to reflect on your personal obstacle?

**THERAPIST-ORIENTED**

# Using Pillar 2 to reflect with a client

1. Ask them to reflect on a personal obstacle (e.g., fear) in the way of what they're wanting for themself.

2. Invite them to choose a specific example of a situation where they experienced this personal obstacle, and see if they're able to unpack the different aspects of this situation that contributed to their distress.

3. Inquire into what they become aware of as they give themself time to reflect on their personal obstacle.

# PILLAR 3:
# Reinforcing Agency

Pillar 3 is about helping a client acknowledge and own their part in the internal dynamics that shape their relationship to Self and others. While external factors lead to complex trauma, most of these external influences we cannot change, as they belong to either the past or larger systemic forces that an individual is generally helpless to change alone. We work on what we can change *within* therapy—and that starts inside the client. Therefore, exploring agency isn't primarily focused on what a client does behaviorally in the external world, but on how a client is organizing and relating to their internal world. As we say in NARM: *"There's what is, and there's what we do to ourselves with what is."*

Although the word *agency* comes from the Latin word meaning "to act," we view agency in terms of how we are actors in our own internal experience. There's a human being mediating external and internal input in a variety of ways, and people are often powerless to change the external factors they face in their lives, but they are not passive in how they relate and respond to life experience. Humans do have the capacity to relate to themselves and the world in ways that support either connection or disconnection. Unlike children, who are 100 percent dependent on their environment for them to feel OK, adults can experience health and well-being amid trying external circumstances. Resilience involves developing a greater sense of security within oneself, which leads to feelings of hopefulness, confidence, and empowerment.

Agency relates to viewing people as complex human beings who are influencing their own physical, emotional, behavioral, and relational experiences. NARM focuses on the adaptations individuals have made in response to traumatic experiences. Exploring agency is about learning how our clients have carried these survival adaptations into their present-day distress and symptoms. Reinforcing agency is about supporting our clients' capacity to become aware of their role in maintaining their distress and symptoms, and helping them shift their relationship to these old adaptive survival patterns. Healing comes as clients gain a felt sense that while they had no agency as a child, they can experience agency in self-supportive ways as an adult.

Agency interventions help clients gain greater awareness of how they are relating to and organizing their life experience, particularly as they explore the obstacles in their way of what they want out of therapy. Agency emerges initially out of the therapeutic contract (Pillar 1). The client fuels the session by connecting to their intention of what they want for themself. The therapist then explores with them how what they say they want for themself is either consistent or inconsistent with how they are leading their life.

For example, a client who wants to feel more confidence in their life is describing an incident at work when their boss gave them constructive feedback that "made me lose my confidence."

THERAPIST: *So I hear that when your boss gave you that feedback, you immediately started attacking yourself—telling yourself that you are a bad employee and always mess things up.*

CLIENT: *You're right. I guess that I do start attacking myself.*

THERAPIST: *How might attacking yourself impact your confidence?*

CLIENT: *If I step back, I can see that this feedback could help me in my job. I can even see that my boss cares about me and wants me to succeed. So attacking myself just gets in my way.*

THERAPIST: *Would it be fair to say that your boss doesn't make you lose your confidence, but you lose your confidence when you attack yourself?*

CLIENT: *Wow, that hits deep. I do this everywhere in my life, and I don't have to do that anymore. I am ready to stop!*

THERAPIST: *To me, that sounds confident.*

In this example, the therapist helps reflect on a pattern of self-attack that is disrupting the client's sense of confidence. Exploring the role this client plays in disconnecting from themselves—through self-attack—helps them better understand a familiar theme in their life. Agency interventions are used to gently highlight the client's role in their suffering, instead of passively experiencing their suffering as coming from the outside, blaming their boss for their loss of confidence. Additionally, agency interventions reinforce connection—through an emerging sense of self-confidence—as the client declares that they don't have to continue self-attacking and are ready to stop this old pattern. This example demonstrates how reinforcing agency creates the possibility for clients to reconnect to themselves through greater understanding, compassion, kindness, and support.

# THERAPEUTIC SHORTCUTS
# FOR PILLAR 3

- Agency is about recognizing and owning one's part in internal and external dynamics.

- Any intervention that supports a client to reflect on how they are relating to their experience is an opportunity for supporting their agency.

- Even when clients can't recognize, or they actively move away from, their capacity for intention and agency, we hold the possibility of increased agency.

- We use language that supports the possibility of increased agency.

- Agency emerges from the therapeutic contract (Pillar 1).

- Client fuels the session by connecting to the intention (Pillar 1) of what they want for themselves.

- We then explore how what they say they want for themself is inconsistent with how they are leading their life.

- Agency interventions exist on a spectrum between invitations for self-reflection and direct confrontation.

- Agency is the opposite of blaming and shaming.

- Healing comes as clients recognize that while they had no agency as a child, they can experience agency as an adult.

- Reinforcing agency relies on the recognition that clients relate to themselves in ways that either support connection or reinforce disconnection.

- Agency supports exploration into the role one plays in disconnecting from one's authentic Self (child consciousness) and reconnecting to one's authentic Self (embodied adult consciousness).

- Agency is the bridge that leads clients from child consciousness to embodied adult consciousness.

# Reinforcing Agency Might Sound Like:

"How are you relating to your family conflict in this moment?"

"What are you telling yourself about this stressful situation?"

"What do you do internally with this information?"

"So when you start to notice your shame, you then shame yourself for that?"

"So when you don't know what to do, you start calling yourself stupid."

"So despite the risks, you asked for what you needed — what do you make of that?"

"I notice you shame yourself when you start to feel and express your anger."

"How are you relating to the way this person is treating you?"

Examples of questions and phrases of Pillar 3

Pillar 3 is about how we look for and reflect back "cracks" in our client's old, familiar patterns of identity and associated survival strategies. Following are some examples of how clients might tell you they experience a sense of increased agency—we invite you to add more that you hear from listening to your clients.

- I can't control others and situations, but I am in charge of how I navigate those people and situations.
- I feel like I am in the driver's seat rather than the backseat.
- I feel much less like a victim and more like the author of my life.
- I am more aware of how I connect and disconnect from what's most authentic in me.
- I no longer feel so helpless and powerless.
- I have choice.

- I am able to accept where I can take action on my own behalf and where I can't.

- I feel an expanded sense of internal capacity.

- Even though things may not be going right, I can still be there for myself.

- I don't have to blame others or shame myself; I can learn from these difficult experiences.

- It feels empowering to feel more "adult" in my life.

- I want to continue learning the ways I am contributing to my own problems.

## EXERCISES

### PERSONAL

## Using Pillar 3 to reflect for yourself

1.  Reflect on something negative you have believed about yourself—for example, you may tell yourself *I am stupid, I am too much,* or *I am unlovable.*

2.  Taking that old belief, turn it into a more active statement—for example, try out *I tell myself that I am stupid, I have the belief that I am too much,* or *I have convinced myself that I am unlovable.*

3.  Notice what it feels like internally to shift these old beliefs into more active statements.

**THERAPIST-ORIENTED**

# Using Pillar 3 to reflect with a client

1.  Ask them about something negative they have believed about themselves—for example, they may tell themselves *I am stupid, I am too much,* or *I am unlovable.*

2.  Support them in turning that old belief into a more active statement—
    for example, they may try out *I tell myself that I am stupid, I have
    the belief that I am too much,* or *I tell myself over and over that I
    am unlovable.*

3.  Inquire into what it feels like internally to shift these old beliefs into
    more active statements.

# PILLAR 4:
# Reflecting Psychobiological Shifts

Pillar 4 supports clients with awareness and an embodied experience of states of reorganization, integration, and transformation. Therapists support their clients to have awareness of the various physical, emotional, cognitive, behavioral, relational, and spiritual shifts that reinforce deepening connection to Self. As the therapist observes and reflects what a client experiences as they move toward greater connection, the therapist also observes and reflects the strategies a client uses to move away from connection. Clients who are invited to reflect on these psychobiological shifts can begin changing their ways of relating to themselves through self-shame, self-judgment, self-attack, and self-hatred (strategies of disconnection) and can start relating to themselves through curiosity, presence, self-acceptance, and self-compassion (states of connection).

Pillar 4 isn't something we specifically do to our clients; it's how the therapist observes, reflects, and reinforces the client's organic movement toward greater connection, regulation, and organization, as well as movement that reinforces disconnection, dysregulation, and disorganization. Clients initially need the therapist's help to learn how to develop this dual awareness, which allows them to track patterns of connection and disconnection. Dual awareness is a pathway to affect regulation. This process supports increased capacity for a client learning to stay present to and contain the often intense feelings they have learned to disconnect from—often referred to as affect tolerance. A client who learns to develop greater affect regulation and tolerance also increases their psychobiological capacity.

Psychobiological shifts are not always so obvious to the client. Without guidance, clients can easily move away from connection to new internal states and back to the adaptive survival strategies they have long used to avoid internal connection. Clients may not be aware of these shifts occurring, and sometimes they actively want to move away from experiencing them because these shifts feel scary. Supporting clients to be present as they are experiencing these psychobiological shifts can lead to a new experience of themselves increasingly free from their adaptive survival patterns. An embodied experience of increasing psychobiological capacity is the manifestation of healing of complex trauma.

For example, a client who has felt helpless and depressed and wants to feel more joy in their life (Pillar 1) shares about feeling more hopeful in their relationship:

THERAPIST: *Would it be OK for you to take a moment to notice what's happening inside as you share that you're feeling more hopeful?*

CLIENT: *I'm not sure I understand your question.*

THERAPIST: *You mentioned that you're feeling more hopeful in your relationship, so I am curious if you're aware of any sensations or emotions you might be having right now.*

CLIENT: *It's always hard for me to feel. It's just something I'm not good at.*

THERAPIST: *Yes, you've shared with me before that you have had a hard time feeling in your life. But in this moment, is it OK to take a little time to see if you can notice what you're feeling?*

CLIENT: *Hmm, I guess so.*

THERAPIST: *As you're taking this time for yourself, what do you notice inside?*

CLIENT: *I guess I kinda feel lighter. It's trippy actually. Like a little disorienting.*

THERAPIST: *Does it feel OK to stay present with your internal feelings in this moment?*

CLIENT: *Yes, it's actually not that bad. I don't know I've felt this before. It feels new.*

THERAPIST: *Can you describe that new feeling?*

CLIENT: *The lightness feels like . . . happiness.*

THERAPIST: *From this place, what's it like to reflect back to your original intention for yourself about feeling more joy in your life?*

CLIENT: *That's right! I do feel more joyful and hopeful right now. And I'm feeling grateful to you for your support. I'm actually feeling very touched [touching their heart].*

Ultimately, a therapist being present to a client's psychobiological shifts reinforces the intersubjective process—how both therapist and client show up in their shared humanity, with heartfulness, that leads to powerful moments of connection, embodiment, depth, and healing.

# THERAPEUTIC SHORTCUTS
# FOR PILLAR 4

- Pillar 4 is about resourcing clients by identifying, reflecting, and reinforcing psychobiological shifts toward greater connection and organization.

- We support dual awareness, which includes the capacity to track states of connection and disconnection.

- We reflect on moments of connection within the context of disconnection strategies.

- We track psychobiological shifts on multiple levels of a client's experience—physical, emotional, cognitive, behavioral, relational, and spiritual.

- Pillar 4 supports awareness of and importance of allowing time for *connection*, *reorganization*, *integration,* and *transformation* into new neural and physiological pathways.

- We support the possibility of increased embodiment when we reflect somatic shifts as they occur.

- When we observe psychobiological shifts, we do not interpret; we simply observe and reflect what we are noticing to the client.

- We reflect psychobiological capacities that are already established as well as those that are still developing.

- Psychoeducation, normalizing, and appropriate self-disclosure are often part of this process.

- After a significant shift that supports increased agency, psychobiological capacity, and disidentification, we may reflect on the original intention (Pillar 1 contract).

- Pillar 4 is about supporting and tracking our clients' capacity to tolerate increasing states of flow, connection, health, and aliveness.

## Reflecting Psychobiological Shifts Might Sound Like:

"I notice you smile as you say that."

"It seems like you are brighter overall —does that resonate with you?"

"I notice you're making more eye contact with me now."

"It looks like your shoulders dropped —what are you noticing in your body right now?"

"It seems like you are experiencing more settling now."

"If it's OK, just take the time you need with what's happening inside."

"I see that you are crying."

"What is it like to take some time with that relief?"

*Examples of questions and phrases of Pillar 4*

Pillar 4 is about identifying, reflecting, and reinforcing psychobiological shifts toward increased connection and organization. Following are some examples of how a therapist might reflect different psychobiological shifts with clients. We invite you to add more possible reflections that you could share with your clients when observing them. Remember, sometimes clients can shift rapidly from connection to disconnection, or from expansion to contraction, and we are not trying to get them to stay in any one place. We are simply wanting to help them be increasingly present and able to contain their full, authentic experience.

- If it's OK, just take all the time you want with what's happening inside.
- Can you share more about your feeling inside?
- I invite you to notice how it is to experience that "good" feeling inside.
- You said you feel more hopeful. What do you notice about that sense of hopefulness inside?

- How is it to notice that sense of relief?
- What's it like to take time with that sense of settling?
- It looked like your shoulders dropped. What are you noticing in your body right now?
- I notice that you smile as you say that.
- I notice you making more eye contact with me now.
- It seems like you are brighter overall—does that resonate for you?
- You were experiencing a settling and now you're experiencing a move back into some worry?
- How is it to be present with your groundedness while you notice some anxiety?
- How is it to stay with both feelings—your hope and your skepticism?
- What's it like to be feeling into what you called your "adult"?
- How is it to feel into this expansiveness?

## EXERCISES

**PERSONAL**

## Using Pillar 4 to reflect for yourself

1. Reflect on a significant shift you've experienced in the course of your own healing and growth.

**2.** How did this shift impact you on all levels of your experience—
physically, emotionally, cognitively, relationally, spiritually?

**3.** What impacts did this shift have on your life in general?

**THERAPIST-ORIENTED**

## Using Pillar 4 to reflect with a client

**1.** Reflect with them on a significant shift they've experienced in the
course of their own healing and growth.

2.   Inquire into how this shift impacted them on all levels of their experience—physically, emotionally, cognitively, relationally, spiritually.

3.   Ask about the impacts this shift has had on their life in general.

# NARM RELATIONAL MODEL
---

## *How internal states inform relational skills*

**The NARM Relational Model** orients around states of *being* within the therapist, and ways of *being* between the therapist and client. This intersubjective model of supporting human-to-human connection is an embodied, dynamic process that is intended to support therapists in showing up with their clients in a way that facilitates therapeutic change.

For sake of clarity, we have deconstructed a holistic interpersonal process into three distinct internal states within the therapist—*curiosity, self-inquiry,* and *presence*—that shape and inform five relational skills: *attunement, acceptance, reflection and exploration, mindful interventions,* and *integration* (see image).

Although we are presenting this relational model in discrete steps, its implementation will be interwoven throughout a session. Just like in learning to play an instrument, there are many things to remember initially, but with more practice, the steps recede into the background and the process flows more organically. We encourage you not to pressure yourself to try and get it "right." Pressure shuts down curiosity, self-inquiry, and presence. Instead, we invite you to receive, to reflect, to learn, to practice, and to trust in the power of relational engagement throughout the therapeutic process.

The NARM Relational Model creates the foundation for the interpersonal process that supports the resolution of complex trauma patterns. These internal states and relational skills inform and guide all the interventions we use in NARM. They are the foundation for profound healing and growth.

# NARM Relational Model
## A foundation of internal states supports relational skills

REFLECTION & EXPLORATION

ACCEPTANCE

MINDFUL INTERVENTIONS

ATTUNEMENT

INTEGRATION

**CURIOSITY**     **SELF-INQUIRY**     **PRESENCE**

The NARM Relational Model

**PERSONAL**

# Using the NARM Relational Model to reflect for yourself

1.  Can you think of a difficult time in your life when you shared with someone and felt met and supported by this person with openness and curiosity?

2.  Can you think of a difficult time in your life when you shared with someone and felt that this person was trying to fix or change you?

3.  What's it like to notice the difference in how it felt between these two experiences?

**THERAPIST-ORIENTED**

# Using the NARM Relational Model to reflect with a client

1.   Reflect with them on a difficult time in their life when they shared with someone and felt met and supported by this person with openness and curiosity.

2.   Inquire about a difficult time in their life when they shared with someone and felt that this person was trying to fix or change them.

3.   Ask them to notice the difference in how it felt between these two experiences.

# Curiosity

## Inquiring into present experience

Cultivating a state of curiosity supports our ability to be open, receptive, flexible, and in a perpetual mode of learning. Curiosity allows us to remain present with complexity. Instead of pressuring ourselves to know it all, or allowing others to put pressure on us, we can simply remain present and receptive to direct experience.

A good starting place is the simple acknowledgment that we truly do not know what our client's inner experience is, and that we will never fully know it. We hold the perspective that therapy is a collaborative, exploratory process, one in which we are being invited into new learning. We are challenged to stay open to a client's complexity and not to reduce the complexity of their experience by attempting to define their inner reality from the outside. In NARM, we support an inside-out learning process that emerges from this open exploration into unchartered territory.

Although we use psychological understanding such as the adaptive survival styles framework to inform the clinical process, curiosity guides our way. At times, this means we as therapists may feel unclear, confused, uncertain, or even lost. In embracing our "not knowing," we might challenge and expand old ways of understanding. We may be surprised by what emerges and gain a new, embodied experience of "knowing."

By meeting a client with curiosity, we are able to not only learn about our client's inner worlds but also be affected by them. Curiosity may give us a clearer sense about what is in their way of living more fully, freely, and healthfully in their present life. As NARM therapists, we set the intention to learn from and about our clients, and to support them in the process of deeper learning about themselves.

**PERSONAL**

# Reflecting on curiosity for yourself

1.  We invite you to reflect on a relational experience where you may feel confused, and what it is like not to try and figure it out, but to simply be curious.

2.  What's it like to allow yourself to not know?

3.  Does being curious and not knowing change your relationship to this experience?

**THERAPIST-ORIENTED**
# Reflecting on curiosity with a client

1.  Reflect with them on a relational experience where they may feel confused, and what it is like not to try and figure it out, but to simply be curious.

2.  Ask them what it's like to allow themselves to not know.

3.  Inquire if being curious and not knowing changes their relationship to this experience.

# Self-Inquiry

## Reflecting into internal experience

Working from a place of internal quietness with clients, even when there is a lot going on during therapy, requires therapists to cultivate an ongoing relationship to their own internal experience as they sit with clients. This self-inquiry process is central in strengthening all relationships.

Especially when working with attachment and relational trauma, therapists must have the capacity to reflect on how they are impacting their clients, as well as how they are being impacted by their clients. Failure to self-reflect often leads to therapeutic misattunement and a poor prognosis for treatment. One major obstacle in the way of self-inquiry and self-reflection is therapeutic countertransference.

Our understanding of countertransference emerged from psychoanalysis, which cautioned against letting a therapist's feelings get entangled with their client's feelings. Since then, there have been many different interpretations of the processes of transference and countertransference. Mostly, countertransference has been viewed as a negative aspect of the therapeutic process. Without having much awareness, therapists can project onto their clients and act out on them in unhelpful and inappropriate ways, even with the best of intentions. While we agree that countertransference can be a major obstacle in therapy, we also see that it can be used mindfully to deepen the therapeutic relationship.

As we are able to stay present and curious to our internal experience—including countertransference reactions we might feel wary about—we can reflect on this as information, where it may be coming from, and how it might inform the way we are relating to ourselves and our clients. Inviting inquiry into what's going on inside us as therapists helps us become more grounded in our connection to our internal feelings and reactions. This can help us shift out of projections and countertransference acting out toward clients, and can support interventions that are aligned to the client sitting in front of us in this very moment. Self-inquiry is an ongoing process that enhances internal states of curiosity and presence for the therapist and supports greater attunement with our clients. In this way, we can use our countertransference reactions as a pathway for increasing self-awareness.

**PERSONAL**

# Reflecting on self-inquiry for yourself

1.  Reflect on an experience of relational difficulty with someone close to you. What's it like to shift your attention from them to your own internal experience?

2.  What do you become aware of as you shift attention from your outer to inner experience?

3.  How does inquiring into your internal experience change the way you relate to yourself and this relational difficulty?

**THERAPIST-ORIENTED**
# Reflecting on self-inquiry with a client

1. Reflect with them on an experience of relational difficulty with someone close to them. What's it like to shift their attention from the other person to their own internal experience.

2. Ask what they become aware of as they shift attention from their outer to inner experience.

3. Ask whether inquiring into their internal experience changes how they relate to themself and this relational difficulty.

# Presence

## Developing the capacity to be in the here and now

Developing stronger therapeutic presence is rooted in curiosity and self-inquiry. To be able to attend to the here-and-now experience of the therapeutic process, therapists need to be able to be present for themselves, as well as present with their clients.

As therapists are able to be more firmly in the present moment as they sit with clients, new information becomes available. NARM relies on a phenomenological approach, which focuses on subjective experience in the here and now. As our clients tell stories from their past or report on troubling symptoms, we are curious about how they are relating to these stories and symptoms in the here and now. We are curious as to what the symptoms are trying to communicate about their present experience. This is an ongoing process of attending to complex dynamics as they emerge in real time.

To track the present-moment experience, therapists must develop the capacity to be in a receptive state. When in an active "doing" state, mediated by the sympathetic nervous system, therapists may miss important elements emerging within the therapeutic process. The internal noise of efforting can become distressing and create confusion for therapists, leading them to overcompensate by compulsively doing whatever they can to be helpful and see themselves as a helpful therapist. This internal noise, and the behavioral strategies that emerge from it, can become a habitual pattern for therapists and interfere in being receptive and present.

When in a receptive "being" state, mediated by the parasympathetic nervous system, therapists may notice important elements emerging, including the somatic and emotional shifts that are central to the therapeutic process. As therapists develop greater capacity to be open, curious, and receptive to these shifts, they feel less compelled to do something with them, and more capable of holding space for these important shifts. This relational space of presence supports therapists to meet clients with acceptance, compassion, and heartfulness.

Developing these relational capacities supports an internal quietness for therapists that allows them to be more receptive to what is happening for their clients, attuned to what might be most useful in their healing process, and ultimately leads to being more effective in resolving old trauma patterns.

**EXERCISES**

**PERSONAL**

# Reflecting on presence for yourself

1. Reflect on a time you felt more fully present with someone. What do you experience as you reflect on that time?

2. What takes you away from being fully present with someone you're close to?

3. How does feeling more fully present change the way you show up in relationship with this person you're close to?

**THERAPIST-ORIENTED**

# Reflecting on presence with a client

1.  Reflect with them on a time that they felt more fully present with someone in their life. What do they experience as they reflect on that time?

2.  Ask what takes them away from being fully present with someone they're close to.

3.  Inquire into how feeling more fully present changes the way the client shows up in relationship with this person they're close to.

# Attunement

## Being responsive to present experience

Attunement is about listening for and feeling into the client's experience. Clinically, therapists attune to the patterns of distress the client is looking to change, as well as their intention for change. The attunement we are describing includes inviting inquiry into layers of internal experience that the client is often not in touch with and may be actively guarding against. It also includes inviting inquiry into a therapist's own sense of receiving this client, including any countertransference reactions, and the relational dynamic between therapist and client. In this first phase of the relational skills, the intention is for therapists to simply experience how it is for them to sit with their client.

Attunement is built upon authentic empathy and describes the relational capacity to be present with and sense into another person's experience. It is the capacity for "feeling with the heart of another" that allows us to be accurately responsive in relationships. An important point to reinforce is that we see inner states as driving behaviors and patterns of distress, and therefore in NARM, we are not attuning to our client's behaviors, we are attuning to our client's inner states.

We recognize that relational attunement is not about "perfect" relational engagement, but about responsiveness. Therapists can take pressure off themselves by not striving to be perfectly attuned to their clients' inner states, and instead focus on staying open, receptive, and responsive. Therapists can practice self-inquiry of the various levels of their own internal experience while they're sitting with clients and notice any impulses, thoughts, judgments, emotional responses, or somatic reactions that might get in their way of being present with their clients. This also includes developing awareness to recognize when they may be misattuned to their clients and finding their way back into relational attunement.

A therapist may be the first person who has ever provided this level of attunement for their client. Therapists are holding space for deeper capacities than even clients may hold for themselves. Therapists hold the possibility for change even when clients lose sight of it. The gift of attunement alone can go a long way in helping clients stop running from themselves, become curious about their inner worlds, and begin to reconnect to their own healing capacities.

**PERSONAL**
# Reflecting on attunement for yourself

1.  Reflect on a relational experience where you felt fully seen, met, and understood by someone. What do you notice as you reflect on that experience?

2.  Reflect on a relational experience where you did not feel seen, met, or understood by someone. What do you notice as you reflect on that experience?

3.  What do you notice about the difference between these two relational experiences?

# Reflecting on attunement with a client

1.  Reflect with them on a relational experience where they felt fully seen, met, and understood by someone. What do they notice as they reflect on that experience?

2.  Reflect with them on a relational experience where they did not feel seen, met, or understood by someone. What do they notice as they reflect on that experience?

3.  Ask what they notice about the difference between these two relational experiences.

# Acceptance

## Holding increasing complexity of experience

The intention of acceptance is to allow for complexity. As humans, we are faced with managing an extremely complex world. We may use our existing knowledge, beliefs, and agendas to manage the complexity of the therapeutic process, but they can also get in the way of therapists being present and open to the direct experience of their clients.

True acceptance is very hard for humans. For therapists, acceptance requires that they recognize and respect the complexity of who their clients are and not reduce their complexity. Many therapists struggle to do this, worried that if they can't understand, they won't be able to help their clients. Acceptance challenges therapists to be in a place of not-knowing, holding space for the client's full experience, relying on curiosity, interest, and patience, and ultimately, trusting the therapeutic process.

To truly understand another's internal world and to support intersubjective healing, a therapist must get comfortable with novel experience, to the best of their abilities. Once they can say "I don't know," they can be open to new learning and greater complexity. A therapist will never fully know their client's internal experience, but they can continue to learn as they deepen into relationship with them, and this ongoing learning provides the ground for relational healing.

Much of the difficulty in staying open to the complexity relates to a therapist's difficulty in accepting their own helplessness; "I don't know" becomes too hard. To successfully meet clients with acceptance, therapists must also be accepting of themselves; this looks like humility. But therapists can get impatient with themselves and with their clients. For example, therapists may become critical of their clients and blame their clients for being resistant or not working hard enough. Therapists may also blame themselves for not doing it right or believe that they should be somewhere further along in the process. If therapists notice impatience, criticism, and other signs of their lack of humility, those are good reminders to practice self-inquiry by reflecting on what is going on inside. Otherwise, therapists run the risk of acting out on clients by using interventions and exercises to make something happen because they don't know what else to do, which can lead to misattunement and even relational rupture.

Allowing for a lack of knowing, and an acceptance of what is, leads to a process of mutual discovery. Being in this learning process with clients is an important step for therapists in connecting deeper with clients, and leads to more successful therapeutic outcomes.

**PERSONAL:**
# Reflecting on acceptance for yourself

1.   Reflect on a part of yourself that you have a hard time accepting.

2.   Reflect on a part of yourself that you once rejected and are now accepting of.

3.   How does acceptance feel, and what helped you to be more self-accepting?

**THERAPIST-ORIENTED:**

# Reflecting on acceptance with a client

1.   Reflect with them on a part of themself that they have a hard time accepting.

2.   Reflect with them on a part of themself that they once rejected and are now accepting of.

3.   Ask them how acceptance feels, and what helped them be more self-accepting.

# Reflection and Exploration

## Developing a working hypothesis

The intention of reflection and exploration is to begin understanding how a client organizes and relates to their inner world. By inviting the client into deeper engagement with their internal world, therapists learn how a client's present life is being impacted by unresolved core dilemmas. These internal conflicts between one's authentic Self and the adaptations they had to make as children drive maladaptive symptoms and lead to lifelong suffering. The relational process of being curious about a client's core dilemma, and how it is impacting their present life, leads to a therapist's working hypothesis.

As therapists explore and ask questions, they are forming an initial understanding about what is keeping a client stuck in their suffering. A working hypothesis is not a strict interpretation that we use to categorize or pathologize clients. Like in the scientific method, our hypothesis fuels further exploration and is subject to continuous revision as more information emerges. There is a constant delivery of information within the therapeutic process, and it is all "grist for the mill."

We are not using this information to solve a puzzle. We want to avoid becoming too goal-oriented around fixing clients. We instead use the wealth of information we receive to deepen our understanding of a client's inner world, how we can meet them where they are, and which interventions may be supportive toward their intended change.

A therapist's working hypothesis starts by understanding the client's intention for change. The therapeutic contract (Pillar 1) guides therapists to explore what is getting in the client's way of actualizing their intention. The organizing theme emerging from the contracting process is focused on the internal conflict between the desire for and fear of what a client most wants. The therapist helps the client uncover both sides of the dilemma—what they desire for themself, and the obstacles in the way of getting what they most desire. This internal conflict becomes the organizing thread of further exploration and the north star of the therapeutic process.

Based on the organizing thread of a client's intention, and underlying core dilemma, a therapist's working hypothesis informs and guides their exploratory questions (Pillar 2), the ways they reinforce agency (Pillar 3), and their reflection of psychobiological shifts (Pillar 4). The working hypothesis also allows therapists to sense into what authentic emotions may be missing from the client's awareness and how to support them in the emotional completion process. For NARM therapists, the working hypothesis—emerging out of ongoing reflection and exploration throughout their clinical work—shapes the direction of their interventions.

**EXERCISES**

**PERSONAL**

# Reflecting and exploration for yourself

1.  Reflect on a challenging aspect of yourself that you constantly work to fix.

2.  What might it be like for you if you don't become goal-oriented around this aspect?

3.  What's it like not to think of yourself as a problem to be solved?

**THERAPIST-ORIENTED**

# Reflecting and exploration with a client

1.  Reflect with them on a challenging aspect of themself that they constantly work to fix.

2.  Ask them what it might be like for them if they don't become goal-oriented around this aspect.

3.  Ask them what it is like not to think of themself as a problem to be solved.

# Mindful Interventions

## Applying attuned relational skills

The intention of mindful interventions is to hold the possibility that clients can begin to relate to themselves in new ways with increased capacity for connection to Self and others. Instead of relating to themselves through the filters of adaptive survival style patterns—based on self-rejection, self-shame, and self-hatred—clients can begin to relate to themselves with greater capacity for openness, curiosity, and eventually self-acceptance and compassion. Ultimately, as a client receives support to address what is in the way of connection to their authentic Self, they begin to build greater psychobiological capacity for healing and growth.

Mindfully applying interventions relates to an intersubjective process that supports therapists, in connection with their intentions and inner world, to stay in relation with their clients' intentions and inner worlds. NARM therapists practice self-inquiry around their use of interventions, and ideally do not use interventions without clarity of their intention.

The "mindful" part of using interventions is evaluating why a therapist is using a specific tool and how it relates to their working hypothesis. NARM therapists do not use interventions to push for outcomes, to caretake, or to protect clients from their internal feelings. NARM therapists are mindful in their use of interventions as they shape them in support of their client's capacity for increasing depth of experience.

Therapists must also be open to relational feedback in response to their use of interventions. Therapists can practice reflecting on the impact of these interventions on their clients through observing and at times asking clients directly. Therapists must always be willing to reevaluate based on new information they are receiving from the client, from their own internal process, and through the therapeutic relationship. We can learn so much by observing how clients use for themselves the interventions we provide.

As therapists explore mindfully with clients, they give themselves permission to slow down, to pause, to reflect, to try new things, to make mistakes, and to learn all along the way. They learn to give themselves permission to be human within their therapeutic role. Centering on their humanness helps therapists create a platform of mindfulness, where interventions can be used thoughtfully and responsively in attuning to the complexity of their clients' internal worlds.

**EXERCISES**

**PERSONAL**

# Reflecting on mindful interventions for yourself

1.  Reflect on a strategy that you've used to try and change yourself that has not worked.

2.  Reflect on your experience when you stopped trying to change yourself in some area of your life.

3.  Reflect on what overall has supported you to experience more depth in yourself.

**THERAPIST-ORIENTED**

# Reflecting on mindful interventions with a client

1.  Reflect with them on a strategy that they've used to try and change themself that has not worked.

2.  Reflect with them on an experience when they stopped trying to change themself in some area of their life.

3.  Ask what overall has supported them to experience more depth in themself.

# Integration

## Building psychobiological capacity

The intention of integration is to support a client's increasing psychobiological capacity, which leads to long-term growth and health. NARM therapists meet their clients from a place of *being*, not primarily focused on the *doing* of therapy, to support a client in actualizing their desired change.

After a successful intervention has been employed, a client commonly experiences some sort of psychobiological shift toward increased organization. For example, clients may report feeling relieved, less burdened, more settled, more relaxed, more balanced, more expansive, more spacious, more clarity, or more engaged with their therapist. Integrating these internal shifts reinforces movement toward greater psychobiological capacity, allowing the client to meet the world with increased presence, engagement, agency, and self-activation.

However, clients may attempt to minimize these shifts by moving quickly past those moments, or disconnecting in other ways. Therapists provide clients with an opportunity to slow this process down to allow for integration. Sometimes it is as simple as asking the client to slow down. At other times, interruption is necessary when clients want to jump to the next thing, without giving any time to let things settle. When clients do begin to take time and space to be with their internal shifts, they may do it in silence. For many clients and therapists alike, silence is uncomfortable, and even excruciating. Therapists still must not push the process just to make something happen. Therapeutic change will be uncomfortable at times.

Slowing down and creating space for silence, reflection, and integration can become major resources for a client who is so used to running from their internal experience. Integration supports the organismic impulse moving toward connection, health, and aliveness and possibilities for reorganization, healing, and transformation.

EXERCISES

**PERSONAL**

# Reflecting on integration for yourself

1.  Reflect on a significant shift you've experienced. What was it like for you to experience this change?

2.  What has gotten in the way of you staying present to this shift?

3.  How has this change impacted your sense of Self, your relationship to your emotions and your body?

**THERAPIST-ORIENTED**

# Reflecting on integration with a client

1. Reflect with them on a significant shift they've experienced—what it was like for them to experience this change.

2. Reflect with them on what has gotten in the way of them staying present to this shift.

3. Ask them how this change has impacted their sense of Self, their relationship to their emotions and their body.

# NARM EMOTIONAL COMPLETION MODEL

## *Supporting the resolution of complex trauma patterns*

**The NARM Emotional Completion Model** supports clients to develop a new relationship to their inner world. Specifically focusing on what is driving affect dysregulation—and leading to difficulties in relationships and Self-concept—NARM therapists help clients *identify their primary emotions, reflect on the emotion's intention,* and *support a new relationship to unresolved emotional conflicts.* Working through unresolved emotional responses in a titrated way allows clients to integrate the powerful energy contained therein and plays a central role in healing complex trauma.

Disconnecting from one's primary emotions is a survival strategy that children use to protect against environmental failure, the pain of heartbreak, and further loss. Many adults are still running away from their emotions. Therefore, healing consists of helping people reconnect to their primary emotions. Primary emotions are authentic, spontaneous expressions of one's inner experience that leads to connection, expansion, and growth. These emotions are not necessarily "positive" or "negative," they are emotions in service of helping us know ourselves and how to interact in the world. Examples of primary emotions are joy, love, fear, anger, and grief. Some traditions and models see the energy inherent in emotions as the fuel for our aliveness. When emotions become shut down, our life energy becomes compromised, leading to various psychobiological symptoms and disorders.

Children learn to disconnect from their primary emotions because they don't have the capacity to tolerate the intense energetics of strong emotions. They fear these feelings will be too much for them, as well as for others. This leads to problems associated with affect tolerance and regulation. Affect regulation—how a child learns to regulate their emotions—is a key feature in secure attachment and adult health. Our internal security is built upon the capacity to regulate both positive and negative emotions. When children aren't raised in an environment with interpersonal regulation, they don't learn self-regulation. Without the confidence that they can handle and modulate their emotional reactions, people cut off from their emotions and tragically spend the rest of their lives disconnecting from their emotions.

When feeling one's primary emotions no longer feels safe, these emotions become split off, repressed, denied, dissociated, displaced, somaticized, and distorted in other harmful ways. As a result, primary emotional responses become embedded in a child's brain and body as incomplete, unresolved emotional communications. As primary emotions become repressed, default emotions take over. Default emotions are familiar, habitual, and automatic emotional reactions that reinforce disconnection, regression, and dysregulation. Common examples we see with clients are chronic anxiety, prolonged grief, guilt, irritability, and defensive anger. Default emotions do not lead to emotional completion; they serve ongoing disconnection from one's authentic internal experience.

| DEFAULT EMOTIONS | PRIMARY EMOTIONS |
| --- | --- |
| Familiar, habitual, automatic | Unfamiliar, authentic, spontaneous |
| Reinforce regression | Support separation-individuation |
| Reinforce superficial emotionality | Increase emotional depth |
| Reinforce helplessness and powerlessness | Support agency and self-activation |
| Somatically tense and/or collapsed | Somatically grounded, relaxed, and/or expansive |
| Generally acted out and acted in | Generally felt in an embodied way |
| Often experienced as uncontained and overwhelming | Often experienced as contained and organizing |
| Often lead to feeling drained and exhausted | Often lead to feeling refreshed and energized |
| Reinforce disconnection, dysregulation, and disorganization | Support connection, regulation, and organization |
| Disrupt psychobiological capacity | Increase psychobiological capacity |
| Reinforce survival-style identifications and child consciousness | Support disidentification and embodied adult consciousness |

The disconnection from emotion creates difficulties for a person moving into adulthood and has a long-term impact on all aspects of their life. Living a full life requires humans to be moved by life experience and guided by primary emotions. It gives us a sense of feeling human. Thus, supporting a client to move from identifying with default emotions toward reconnecting to their primary emotions is an essential element in resolving complex trauma.

The NARM Emotional Completion Model consists of a three-step process for reconnecting to primary emotions and increasing affect regulation. This approach works directly with internal states, not behaviors, and therefore focuses on emotional containment, not expression. NARM's containment approach strengthens a client's capacity for processing affective and somatic states. Clients learn to be present to internal states without feeling compelled to act them in or act them out. This focus on regulation is the containment process—learning to acknowledge one's primary emotions, understand what they are communicating, and integrate the emotional energy. In this way, working through incomplete emotional responses left unresolved from earlier in life allows clients to experience increased affect regulation in their present life—which leads to stronger relationships and Self-concept.

## The Emotional Completion Model

STEP 2
Reflect on the
Emotion's Intention

STEP 1
Identify the
Primary Emotion

STEP 3
Support a New
Relationship
with
Unresolved
Emotions

Three steps of the NARM Emotional Completion Model

To give a sense of how the Emotional Completion Model looks with clients, here is a short exchange between a NARM therapist and client. In this example, the therapeutic contract (Pillar 1) was that the client wants to feel peace in their relationship but has been feeling shut down and afraid of their emotions. This has led to the client feeling hopeless, depressed, and resigned to a "toxic" relationship.

THERAPIST: *I hear you're feeling mistreated by your partner, and bad about yourself, but I also heard you say that you are feeling a bit annoyed with him?*

[Step 1: inquiring about their annoyance]

CLIENT: *I guess so. But we both know that I end up blaming myself.*

THERAPIST: *Yes, I know that's the historical pattern. But in this moment, is it OK to acknowledge your annoyance?*

[Step 1: acknowledging their annoyance]

CLIENT: *Uh, not sure, I guess. I mean, it truly has been frustrating.*

THERAPIST: *What does your annoyance and frustration want to communicate about your relationship?*

[Step 2: reflecting on the intention of their primary emotions; what is their annoyance and frustration attempting to convey?]

CLIENT: *Interesting question. I suppose . . . that it's not fair. I shouldn't be treated this way. It's just not OK!*

THERAPIST: *What's it like to say that?*

[Step 3: inviting presence with their primary emotions]

CLIENT: *It feels kinda empowering actually.*

THERAPIST: *How is it to be with that empowering feeling in your body?*

[Step 3: inviting containment with their primary emotions]

CLIENT: *I feel stronger. Like I have more energy in my body, but not overwhelming energy, empowering energy.*

THERAPIST: *So as you connect to your annoyance and frustration, you feel stronger and empowered. Would it be OK to take time to be with how this feels inside?*

[Step 3: supporting integration of their primary emotions]

CLIENT: *Yes . . . It feels empowering. And it's strange, because now as I'm thinking about my relationship, I'm actually feeling more peaceful.*

After years of disconnection, embodying and integrating one's primary emotions changes one's relationship with the Self. As clients increase their capacity for tolerating affect, they are more able to stay present with all their feelings without feeling overwhelmed and needing to disconnect. As therapists support clients in building greater capacity for being present with the "positive" feelings of expansion, excitement, joy, gratitude, and love, clients are also developing greater capacity for being present with the "negative" feelings of contraction, distress, rage, grief, and pain. This self-regulatory capacity to be connected to their full range of authentic emotional states leads to increasing states of internal balance, security, and well-being.

## EXERCISES

### PERSONAL
## Reflecting on emotional completion for yourself

1. Reflect on a difficult life experience and what emotions you were feeling in response to this experience.

2. What might've your emotions been attempting to communicate about this difficult experience?

3. What's it feel like internally as you stay present to this reflection on your emotions in response to this difficult experience?

**THERAPIST-ORIENTED**

# Reflecting on emotional completion with a client

1.  Ask them to reflect on a difficult life experience and what emotions they were feeling in response to this experience.

2.  Inquire into what their emotions might've been attempting to communicate about this difficult experience.

3.  Reflect on how it is for them to stay present to this reflection on their emotions in response to this difficult experience.

# Emotional Completion Model—Step 1

## Identifying Primary Emotions

The first step in the emotional completion process is about psychological ownership—in other words, supporting a client to be present with, and not run from, their primary emotions. People use numerous strategies to avoid feeling their authentic feelings. Therefore, helping clients identify and acknowledge a primary emotion is an important first step.

Therapists invite clients to recognize the primary emotion they are feeling. It could be as simple as asking: "What emotion are you aware of right now?" Remember that for a child it is safer to not feel than to feel, so people learn avoidance strategies for feeling, which are now impacting their adult lives. Although this first step might sound simple, in practice a therapist often inquires multiple times to help their clients identify a primary emotion they are experiencing. For example, after several attempts, the therapist might say: "I notice you keep describing your reactions to this experience, but are you able to notice what you are feeling?"

A common strategy clients use to disconnect from and protect against primary emotions is reacting with old, familiar emotional reactions (default emotions). For example, a client who truly feels sad instead blames others, or a client who truly feels angry instead cries hopelessly. NARM therapists explore the possibility that there may be other emotions available besides those that feel most familiar and automatic. Without leading them into any specific emotion, we simply inquire as to any other emotion that may be less obvious to the client. This could look as simple as "You said you have been agitated and reactive at work, and I wonder if you might notice any other emotions associated with what's been happening for you at work?"

Initially, clients may find it challenging to reflect on their primary emotions. Because these avoidant behaviors and default emotions can be so strong, therapists must support clients in gaining awareness of how they disconnect from their primary emotions. Therapists might reflect something like "I notice that every time you begin talking about your ex-partner you either blame them or blame yourself. If you weren't blaming yourself or your partner, what feeling do you think you might feel?"

Although NARM therapists don't push for emotional feeling and expression, they also don't want to collude with clients in moving away from their emotions. The question NARM therapists are considering: *Does this emotion seem to be leading to increased connection (primary emotions) or reinforcing strategies of disconnection (default emotions)?* In other words: *Does this emotion seem to be leading to the possibility of emotional completion?*

The first big step toward integrating once-threatening primary emotions is for clients to connect to their internal experience through openness, interest, and curiosity, as opposed to a goal-driven process of making something happen, changing it, or fixing it.

By simply acknowledging their relationship to primary emotions, clients begin to get the sense that their deepest emotions do not have to feel so scary and overwhelming but can in fact be experienced as liberating, enlivening, and empowering.

## EXERCISES

**PERSONAL**

# Reflecting on step 1 of the Emotional Completion Model for yourself

1.   Reflect on a conflict you have had with a close person in your life that does not feel resolved.

2.   What emotions in particular have not been fully dealt with?

3.   How is it to allow yourself to acknowledge these unresolved emotions in present time?

**THERAPIST-ORIENTED**

# Reflecting on step 1 of the Emotional Completion Model with a client

1.  Reflect with them on a conflict they had with a close person in their life that does not feel resolved.

2.  Ask them what emotions in particular have not been fully dealt with.

3.  Ask them how it is to allow themself to acknowledge these unresolved emotions in present time.

# Emotional Completion Model—Step 2

## Communication of Primary Emotions

The second step in the emotional completion process is about understanding the implicit intention of a client's primary emotion. NARM therapists reflect on these questions: *What is the underlying intention in this emotional response? What message is the emotion attempting to convey? What is the emotion trying to accomplish?*

In this second step, therapists inquire into what it is that the client's primary emotion is trying to communicate. NARM therapists do not assume they know what may be driving a client's emotional response. They stay curious in order to learn.

Therapists invite reflection on the underlying intention in their primary emotion (as identified through step 1). There is an implicit intention in every emotion. Emotional responses serve as both messages to the environment and a message to the Self. For children, expressing emotion is a way of communicating to others about their basic needs. A crying baby may be calling for attention from caregivers about a basic need that requires adult attention. For adults, emotions reinforce connection to one's authentic Self. For example, knowing that we're feeling angry about a situation informs us that something isn't right for us in this situation; the message to Self might be "I don't deserve to be treated this way." Creating space for the intention of our primary emotions leads to healthier ways of feeling into and sharing our emotional responses.

For example, if a client identifies that they feel angry about something in their relationship, the therapist may ask: "What is it that the anger might want to say?" Or with a client who identifies that they feel sad about not being invited to an event, the therapist may ask: "What might the sadness want to communicate?" Or if a client is acting out an emotion in some way—for example, screaming in rage or crying in grief—a therapist might ask: "If the rage/grief had words, what would it say?"

As clients connect to the intention of their primary emotions, they embody a different emotional sense: that their emotions are valid, genuine, and important. This embodied experience helps clients complete unresolved emotional responses left over from earlier in their life, and they can begin to experience an increasing sense of confidence, possibility, and internal freedom.

**EXERCISES**

**PERSONAL**

# Reflecting on step 2 of the Emotional Completion Model for yourself

1.    Reflect on someone in your life you may be irritated or angry with.

2.    What might your anger be trying to communicate to the other person?

3.    What might your anger be trying to communicate to yourself?

# Reflecting on step 2 of Emotional Completion Model with a client

1.  Reflect with them about someone in their life they may be irritated or angry with.

2.  Ask them what the anger is wanting to communicate to the other person.

3.  Ask them what the anger is trying to communicate to themself.

# Emotional Completion Model—Step 3

## Integrating Primary Emotions

The third step in the emotional completion process supports clients in learning to integrate the powerful life energy inherent in primary emotions. The emotional completion process is containment based, meaning therapists support clients to stay present to their primary emotions in an embodied way. This approach focuses on providing new ways of relating to one's internal states that generate increased psychobiological capacity.

NARM therapists differentiate between emotional expression and emotional containment, and we generally do not use interventions that encourage emotional expression, discharge, or catharsis. Although emotionally cathartic approaches can be effective at helping clients directly express emotions, they are often not effective at helping clients contain and integrate their emotions and build increased capacity for affect regulation. The irony is that as clients integrate the energy inherent in their emotions—as opposed to focusing on its expression—they often experience new possibilities for how to more authentically express their primary emotions.

Therapeutic interventions such as slowing down, practicing somatic mindfulness, and inviting the naming of internal states help clients learn to tolerate the expansion that comes with feeling their primary emotions. It may be as simple as asking, "Is it OK for you to be with the grief for a moment?" At other times, therapists may be more specific in their questions—for example, "What are you noticing in your internal experience as you give yourself this time to feel into your grief?" And sometimes therapists may be very specific: "You mentioned that it actually feels good to feel your grief. What exactly is it that you're feeling in your body that 'feels good?'"

Even if a client is only able to stay present with their feelings for a brief moment, these moments of being present with primary emotions in an embodied way lead to increased affect tolerance. Therapists can reflect this back, for example: "I notice that you are able to sit with your anger longer than you used to. What's it like to sit with your anger without needing to so quickly move away from it?" This deeper capacity for tolerating a wide range of affects, including being with complex and even conflicting emotional states, leads to improvements in affect regulation, a core aspect of overall health and well-being.

Completion does not imply that these emotions are finished or go away. In fact, it's quite the opposite. The emotional completion process provides clients with an inner knowing that they can stay present to their emotional responses—even intense and powerful ones. As clients are able to connect to their primary emotions and what they are trying to affect, core expressions of their life force that had been bound up in old adaptive survival-style patterns become available. Instead of channeling life energy into long-standing strategies and symptoms, they have direct access to their life energy for use in self-supportive ways. Clients begin to experience an enhanced capacity for inner states of aliveness, pleasure, creativity, play, gratitude, compassion, and intimacy. As individuals reconnect to their heart and emotions, love for Self and others becomes foundational.

## EXERCISES

### PERSONAL
## Reflecting on step 3 of the Emotional Completion Model for yourself

1. Reflect on an emotional response that doesn't feel resolved.

2. See if you are able to give yourself internal permission to be with this emotion.

3. What's it like to notice the response in your body as you allow yourself to feel this emotion?

**THERAPIST-ORIENTED**

# Reflecting on step 3 of the Emotional Completion Model with a client

1. Reflect with them on an emotional response that doesn't feel resolved.

2. Ask them if they are able to give themself internal permission to be with this emotion.

3. Ask them what it's like to notice the response in their body as they allow themselves to feel this emotion.

# NARM PERSONALITY SPECTRUM MODEL

## *Assessing capacities of Self-organization*

When working with clients who have experienced complex trauma, therapists benefit from having a clinical framework that allows them to understand the psychobiological capacities of their clients. These capacities are foundational elements of the Self. Our personality spectrum model uses a psychobiological perspective for understanding and assessing Self-organization. By using ten specific psychobiological traits, the NARM Personality Spectrum provides a roadmap for identifying where our clients are on the spectrum from the ranges of Organized Self to Adaptive Self to Disorganized Self.

**Organized Self** ⟷ **Adaptive Self** ⟷ **Disorganized Self**

The NARM Personality Spectrum recognizes the link between unresolved developmental trauma and levels of disruption to Self-organization; additionally, this model recognizes the link between the resolution of developmental trauma and levels of increasing Self-organization. Clients with greater levels of Self-disorganization ("Disorganized Self") will require a different approach to treatment than clients with greater levels of Self-organization ("Organized Self"). So the earlier a therapist is able to assess the client's level of internal organization, the more realistic and responsive they can be to the client's capacities, and therefore the more effective they can be in treatment.

The NARM Personality Spectrum provides a way of understanding a client's inner world, including the disorganization of psychobiological states that drive the symptoms of C-PTSD, including affect dysregulation, negative self-concept, and interpersonal disturbances. We are attempting to identify and assess our client's capacity, so as to gain greater awareness of the internal dynamics leading to a client's symptoms and distress. This map helps therapists individualize their therapeutic interventions in relation to where their clients fall along the personality spectrum.

Thus, the NARM Personality Spectrum is intended to create a clear picture of where the client is in the moment regarding their ability to engage with and benefit from the therapeutic process. Identifying the range of a client's Self-organization helps answer the question *Does this client have the capacity to benefit from the intervention that I think might be a good one for them right now?*

What are the core psychobiological traits shaped through childhood that we are using to better understand a client's health? While not an exhaustive list, the ones we use help capture essential traits that represent the characteristics of an individual's Self-organization and how this gets expressed through personality.

**Connection:** Capacity for connection to oneself and others

**Separation-Individuation:** Capacity for differentiation, independence, adult consciousness

**Self-Regulation:** Capacity to regulate one's internal states

**Agency:** Capacity to experience ownership for one's life

**Capacity for Intimacy/Therapeutic Alliance:** Capacity to experience others as a source of support

**Empathy:** Capacity to relate to the internal world of others

**Self-Awareness/Insight:** Capacity for inquiry and self-discovery

**Consensus Reality:** Capacity to experience life with minimal projections

**Self-Activation:** Capacity to initiate and set the course for one's life

**Presence:** Capacity for embodied living in the here and now

# 10 PSYCHOBIOLOGICAL TRAITS

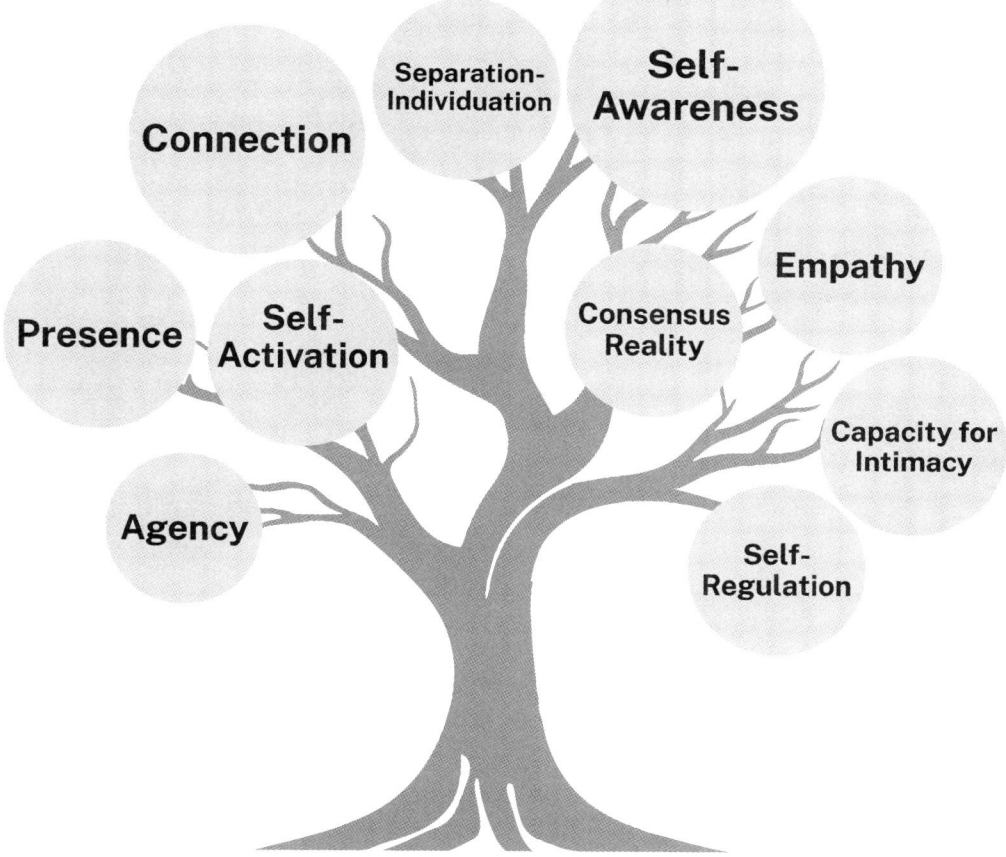

Ten psychobiological traits of the NARM Personality Spectrum

The NARM Personality Spectrum helps therapists gauge progress as they support their clients toward increasing psychobiological capacity—tracking the movement from Self-disorganization toward increasing Self-organization. For clients with internal disorganization, these ten traits are disrupted, which leads to symptoms associated with C-PTSD. As internal organization develops, these ten traits work in coherence, supporting the internal states conducive to health, well-being, and aliveness.

**PERSONAL**

# Reflecting on the NARM Personality Spectrum for yourself

1. Which of these ten psychobiological traits do you feel is the most developed in you?

2. Which of these ten psychobiological traits do you feel is the least developed in you?

3. Which of these ten psychobiological traits have you most strengthened in your own healing and growth?

**THERAPIST-ORIENTED**

# Reflecting on the NARM Personality Spectrum with a client

1. Ask them which of these ten psychobiological traits they feel is the most developed in them.

2. Ask them which of these ten psychobiological traits they feel is the least developed in them.

3. As them which of these ten psychobiological traits they have most strengthened in their healing and growth.

# NARM PERSONALITY SPECTRUM WORKSHEET

We invite you to use the NARM Personality Spectrum worksheet on the following pages to score a client on each of the ten psychobiological traits, and then add up the final score (from 10 to 100) using the rubric on page 135.

After scoring, you're invited to reflect on:

- What's your overall sense looking at your client through this lens?

- What might this suggest about treatment?

- What might this suggest about prognosis?

- What other support may be indicated?

- How might this relate to your work with this client?

- How might this relate to your feeling about your client?

- How might this relate to how you view yourself as a therapist?

# NARM Personality Spectrum Worksheet

Choose a client and fill out the spectrum below.
Circle one along the spectrum: 10 (very high) to 1 (very low)

| Psychobiological Traits | Organized Self | | | Adaptive Self | | | Disorganized Self | | |
|---|---|---|---|---|---|---|---|---|---|
| **1. Connection**<br>capacity for connection to oneself and others | 10 | 9 | 8 | 7 | 6 | 5 | 4 | 3 | 2 | 1 |
| **2. Separation-Individuation**<br>capacity for differentiation, independence, and adult consciousness | 10 | 9 | 8 | 7 | 6 | 5 | 4 | 3 | 2 | 1 |
| **3. Self-Regulation**<br>capacity to regulate one's internal states | 10 | 9 | 8 | 7 | 6 | 5 | 4 | 3 | 2 | 1 |
| **4. Agency**<br>capacity to take ownership for one's life | 10 | 9 | 8 | 7 | 6 | 5 | 4 | 3 | 2 | 1 |
| **5. Capacity for Intimacy/ Therapeutic Alliance**<br>capacity to experience others as a source of support | 10 | 9 | 8 | 7 | 6 | 5 | 4 | 3 | 2 | 1 |
| **6. Empathy**<br>capacity to relate to the internal world of others | 10 | 9 | 8 | 7 | 6 | 5 | 4 | 3 | 2 | 1 |
| **7. Self-Awareness/Insight**<br>capacity for inquiry and self-discovery | 10 | 9 | 8 | 7 | 6 | 5 | 4 | 3 | 2 | 1 |
| **8. Consensual Reality**<br>capacity for experiencing life with minimal projections | 10 | 9 | 8 | 7 | 6 | 5 | 4 | 3 | 2 | 1 |
| **9. Self-Activation**<br>capacity to initiate and set the course for one's life | 10 | 9 | 8 | 7 | 6 | 5 | 4 | 3 | 2 | 1 |
| **10. Presence**<br>capacity to be in the here and now (present moment) | 10 | 9 | 8 | 7 | 6 | 5 | 4 | 3 | 2 | 1 |

**TOTAL SCORE (out of 100)**

*Please note: The NARM Personality Spectrum is not an evidence-based diagnostic mechanism. It is an assessment tool that can support mental health professionals in reflecting on their clients. The scoring range provides therapists with a framework for assessing Self-Organization: where clients are on a range from greater organization (Organized Self), to less organization/more disorganization (Adaptive Self), to significant disorganization (Disorganized Self). Additionally, we have found that clients enjoy learning about themselves through the NARM Personality Spectrum. We hope that it can also support personal growth for those who are interested in using it in this way.*

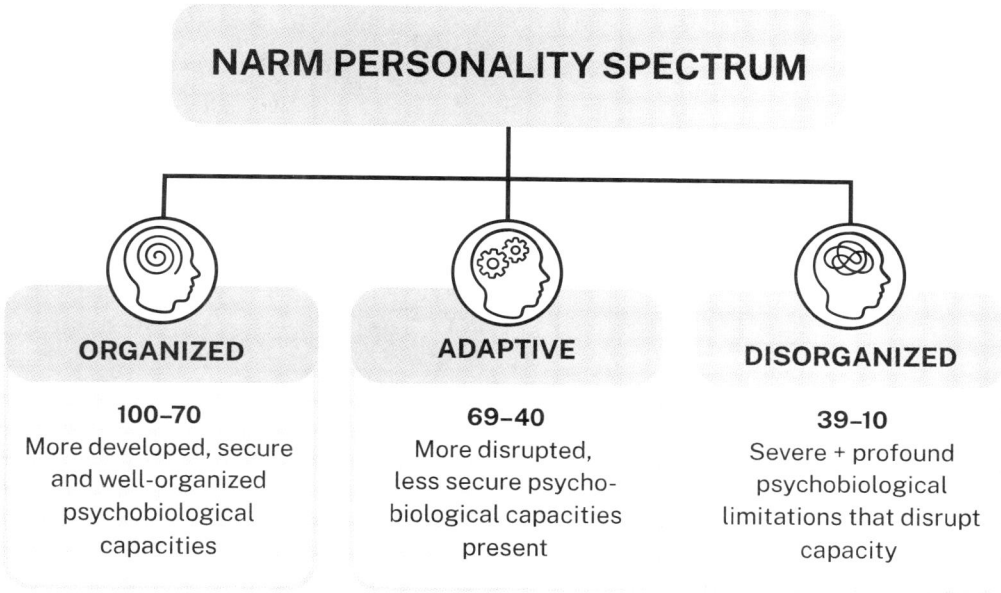

The NARM Personality Spectrum scoring ranges

## SCORING RANGE

### 100–70: ORGANIZED SELF RANGE

Clients in this range may have more developed, secure, and well-organized psychobiological capacities that lead to them moving through their lives with greater flexibly and resiliency. Their coping strategies tend to be more on the healthy, mindful side—things like exercise, healthy eating, social engagement, and just a general self-care orientation. Their observing ego is stronger, with greater capacity for self-reflection, self-awareness, self-insight, self-agency, and self-activation. Therapeutically, there tends to be very good prognosis for treatment. These clients are more open, engaged, and collaborative, and they engage with the therapist in the spirit of goodwill. The therapeutic process is often enriching for both client and therapist.

## 69–40: ADAPTIVE SELF RANGE

Clients in this range may have more disrupted, less secure psychobiological capacities that lead to them moving through their lives experiencing frequent challenge, distress, and symptoms. These clients often experience various psychobiological symptoms and disorders. Their coping strategies tend to be more problematic, and though they may experience some sense of flexibility and resiliency, they often get in their own way of self-activation, success, and fulfillment in multiple areas of their lives. Their observing ego is weaker, with compromised capacity for self-reflection, self-awareness, self-insight, and self-agency. Therapeutically, at least initially, there tends to be a good to fair prognosis for treatment. These clients are more challenging, in both their capacity to use the therapeutic skills and their engagement with the therapist. The therapeutic process may at times be quite challenging and frustrating for both client and therapist.

## 39–10: DISORGANIZED SELF RANGE

Clients in this range may have severe and profound psychobiological limitations that disrupt their ability to move through their lives without experiencing consistent challenge and distress. These clients are often desperately seeking help while at the same time feeling frustrated and unsatisfied at receiving the help they are getting; they often dismiss, minimize, or outright reject support. Their coping strategies are limited in general, and they tend to act in and act out, at times in ways that can be off-putting, threatening, and even dangerous for themselves and others. They tend not to experience a sense of flexibility and resiliency and may disrupt movement toward self-activation, success, and fulfillment in multiple areas of their lives. They do not experience an observing ego and have impaired capacity for self-reflection, self-awareness, self-insight, and self-agency. Therapeutically, at least initially, there tends to be a fair to poor prognosis for treatment. These clients have limited capacity overall, may express resistance to using therapeutic skills for themselves, and may engage with the therapist in a challenging, adversarial, or even threatening manner. The therapeutic process may be extremely challenging, frustrating, and troubling for both client and therapist.

One important additional note about clients in the Disorganized Self range: Clients are humans, and even when they are struggling with a poor prognosis and limitations in multiple areas of their lives, we stay committed to them receiving the most optimal care. Because someone is experiencing more limitation in their present life does not mean anything negative about the person or about their potential for healing and growth. As human beings, we are all struggling to some degree. We want to remember that a client's disorganization and symptoms do not define the person. The person sitting in front of us is so much more than these symptoms and their suffering. We always meet our clients holding dual awareness—the reality of the level of their challenges (using the NARM Personality Spectrum to assess) as well as the hope for them to heal (using the NeuroAffective Relational Model to treat). We hope that therapists keep in mind that the NARM Personality Spectrum is a tool for humanizing our clients' experience. We hope that this tool for identifying our clients' present capacity can help us provide more effective treatment for all our clients.

# CONCLUSION

We hope you can use this workbook to enhance your effectiveness in healing complex trauma. Our vision was to find a way to present a sophisticated therapeutic model in an easy-to-apply format, so as to make this healing work more accessible to people in need. We hope that you keep this workbook close as you begin to apply NARM, and continue returning to this resource in support of your professional development—and perhaps your own personal growth as well.

As you begin experimenting with the NARM skills provided in this workbook, it is likely that you will recognize that it is impossible to fully integrate a comprehensive clinical model through a book. If you're finding NARM to be useful, or at least worthy of further investigation, there are other resources, learning programs, and clinical trainings available to deepen your understanding of the NeuroAffective Relational Model (see "Additional Resources," p. 143).

It is our intention for NARM to contribute to the trauma-informed movement as it reaches more mental health and other helping professionals. We believe that NARM can play an important role in supporting personal, therapeutic, and collective change. Our aspiration is that NARM can lead to increasing opportunities for connection, healing, and transformation in individuals, relationships, communities, and society. We truly hope that in some small way, this workbook will support this movement.

Transforming trauma is a journey. It is our heart's desire that the NeuroAffective Relational Model can support you and your clients along your journey.

## CONCLUSION EXERCISES

1.   How might you use NARM to support your professional work?

- In terms of your impact as a helping professional, what would you ike to happen?

- Wha is your heart's desire?

2.   How might you use NARM to support your personal growth?

- In terms of impact on your own life, what would you like to happen?

- What is your heart's desire?

3.  What do you notice internally as you reflect on your learning of NARM?

- We encourage you to take your time to reflect on your body, emotions, thoughts, and any other internal experience.

- What do you notice in your heart?

# ADDITIONAL RESOURCES

We hope that this book has inspired you to learn more!

For additional learning resources, we encourage you to visit the websites of both the NARM Training Institute and the Complex Trauma Training Center to learn more about the resources, webinars, trainings, programs, and events they offer to helping professionals:

**NARM Training Institute**: www.narmtraining.com

**Complex Trauma Training Center**: www.complextraumatrainingcenter.com

We invite you to listen to the CTTC podcast *Transforming Trauma*: www.complex traumatrainingcenter.com/transformingtrauma

We encourage you to read the two NARM books:

*Healing Developmental Trauma: How Early Trauma Affects Self-Regulation, Self-Image, and the Capacity for Relationship* by Dr. Laurence Heller and Dr. Aline LaPierre

*The Practical Guide for Healing Developmental Trauma: Using the NeuroAffective Relational Model to Address Adverse Childhood Experiences and Resolve Complex Trauma* by Dr. Laurence Heller and Brad Kammer, LMFT, LPCC

# FURTHER STUDY IN THE NEUROAFFECTIVE RELATIONAL MODEL

**The NARM® Training Institute** is an educational organization created to support mental health and helping professionals who work with the impacts of developmental and complex trauma. Our mission is to humanize and depathologize mental health and other professional helping fields, and our trainings reflect that.

NARM teaches a significant new perspective on both the development and treatment of complex trauma (C-PTSD), which integrates attachment understanding, a non-Western orientation to identity, and an evidence-based understanding of the body and the nervous system. Our trainings teach participants to address symptoms, not simply to extinguish them, and more importantly, to address what is driving them. Our trainings and resources are designed to educate and train professionals while providing a different perspective on trauma-informed services. Our programs include entry- and senior-level training programs, ongoing learning through our Inner Circle membership, and other supplemental learning options.

To learn more, please visit the website www.narmtraining.com.

**The Complex Trauma Training Center (CTTC)** offers training and consultation for mental health professionals working with individuals and communities impacted by adverse childhood experiences (ACEs) and complex trauma (C-PTSD).

Our intention is to provide a relational, diverse, inclusive, depth-oriented professional community for those seeking a supportive network of therapists.

We offer clinical trainings in integrative modalities that are effective for C-PTSD as well as professional programs that support therapists in working with a diverse range of clients.

CTTC hosts clinical trainings in the NeuroAffective Relational Model® (NARM®), offering both NARM® Therapist and NARM® Master Therapist trainings online, in-person, and hybrid format.

CTTC also hosts SPACE: An Inner Development Program of Support and Self-Discovery for Therapists on the Personal, Interpersonal, and Transpersonal Levels. SPACE is an online program for Supporting Presence, Awareness, Connection, and Embodiment for mental health professionals.

CTTC's mission is to provide ongoing development and mentorship for clinicians. We believe that increasing effectiveness as therapists is a professional and personal journey that includes clinical training, mentorship, consultation, community engagement, and personal support toward increasing well-being and fulfillment.

If you are interested in learning more about our *clinical trainings*, *ongoing professional development programs*, and *community events*, please visit the website www.complextraumatrainingcenter.com.

# About the Authors

**LAURENCE HELLER, PhD,** holds a doctorate in clinical psychology. He was in private practice for forty years. He developed the NeuroAffective Relational Model (NARM), which is taught throughout the world. He is the author of four books, including *Healing Developmental Trauma*, which has been published in seventeen languages, and coauthor of *The Practical Guide for Healing Developmental Trauma*. He is the founder of NARM and director of the NARM Training Institute and teaches regularly in the US and Europe. Dr. Heller has conducted NARM trainings and case consultations for thousands of therapists throughout the United States and Europe.

www.drlaurenceheller.com

**BRAD KAMMER, LMFT, LPCC,** is the founder and director of the Complex Trauma Training Center. He is a Senior Trainer in NARM and the coauthor of *The Practical Guide for Healing Developmental Trauma*. Brad also developed and teaches the SPACE Program: An Inner Development Program of Support and Self-Discovery for Therapists. Brad began his career as a humanitarian aid worker in Asia working with personal and collective trauma. He is passionate about helping resolve the widespread impact of adverse childhood experiences (ACEs) and complex trauma (C-PTSD). His work is based on the integration of somatic psychology, interpersonal neurobiology, and wisdom from spiritual traditions and traditional cultures. He is a somatically oriented psychotherapist in private practice, professor, producer of the Transforming Trauma podcast, consultant, and international trainer on trauma-informed care.

www.body-mindtherapy.com

# About North Atlantic Books

North Atlantic Books (NAB) is an independent, nonprofit publisher committed to a bold exploration of the relationships between mind, body, spirit, and nature. Founded in 1974, NAB aims to nurture a holistic view of the arts, sciences, humanities, and healing. To make a donation or to learn more about our books, authors, events, and newsletter, please visit www.northatlanticbooks.com.